INTRODUCTION

Welcome to my world.   I have been doing beadwork since 1979.
I have been a craftsperson since 1983 and a teacher of beadwork since 1985.
In that time I have had opportunities to create and see many beadwork pieces
ranging from simple earrings to complicated collars.   Every piece is unique.
Think of your different colored hanks of beads as tubes of oil paint and yourself
as an artist in front of an empty canvas.   A piece of yourself goes into every
one of your creations.   Talk to any bead artist and they will tell you the same
thing.

There are many 'how to' books on the market these days on every subject and
beading is no exception.   So, why one more?   Many beading books I have
bought were difficult to understand and incompletely or poorly illustrated.
In discussing this problem with other bead artists, I found that most agreed that
the beading books available on the market were a disappointment.   I needed
teaching materials for my beadwork classes at a local university so I developed
my own diagrams and instructions for some of the popular stitches.   My
husband does computer-aided graphic design and he offered to work up the
diagrams for my teaching aids.   The results went far beyond my expectations.
My classes reacted so positively to these materials that I decided to market them
to the public.

If you are interested in loomwork, I recommend "Those Bad, Bad Beads" by
Virginia Blakelock. You can find out about costs and how to obtain it by writing
to Virginia Blakelock - 16510 West Edminston Road - Wilsonville, OR 97070.

If you are a newcomer to beadwork, I hope the following pages are helpful.
If you are already a bead artist, I hope you can appreciate the time and work
spent on them.

Desireé Vinson

Corvallis, Oregon
August, 1988

HOW TO USE THIS BOOK

Each of the chapters in this book is designed to stand alone. The first chapter covers basic beading techniques and supplies. If this is your first experience with beadwork you should start there. The second chapter shows six different techniques for adding fringe. Chapters Three through Nine contain instructions for specific stitches.

Although everybody differs in how hard they find a particular stitch to do, the stitches have been ordered loosely from easier (Chevron and Daisy chain) to harder (Commanche stitch and Mexican Lace).

It is **VERY IMPORTANT** that you read a chapter **ALL THE WAY THROUGH** before you actually try out the stitch. This will help you to understand and visualize the stitch. Using contrasting bead colors for your first attempt at the stitch will also help with your visualization.

ACKNOWLEDGMENTS

I would like to say thank you to all the people who made this book possible; My husband, Greg, and his computer, the OSU Craft Center for their blind faith in my ability, and all the students who took classes from me and were willing guinea pigs.

TABLE of CONTENTS

TABLE of CONTENTS

CHAPTER 1

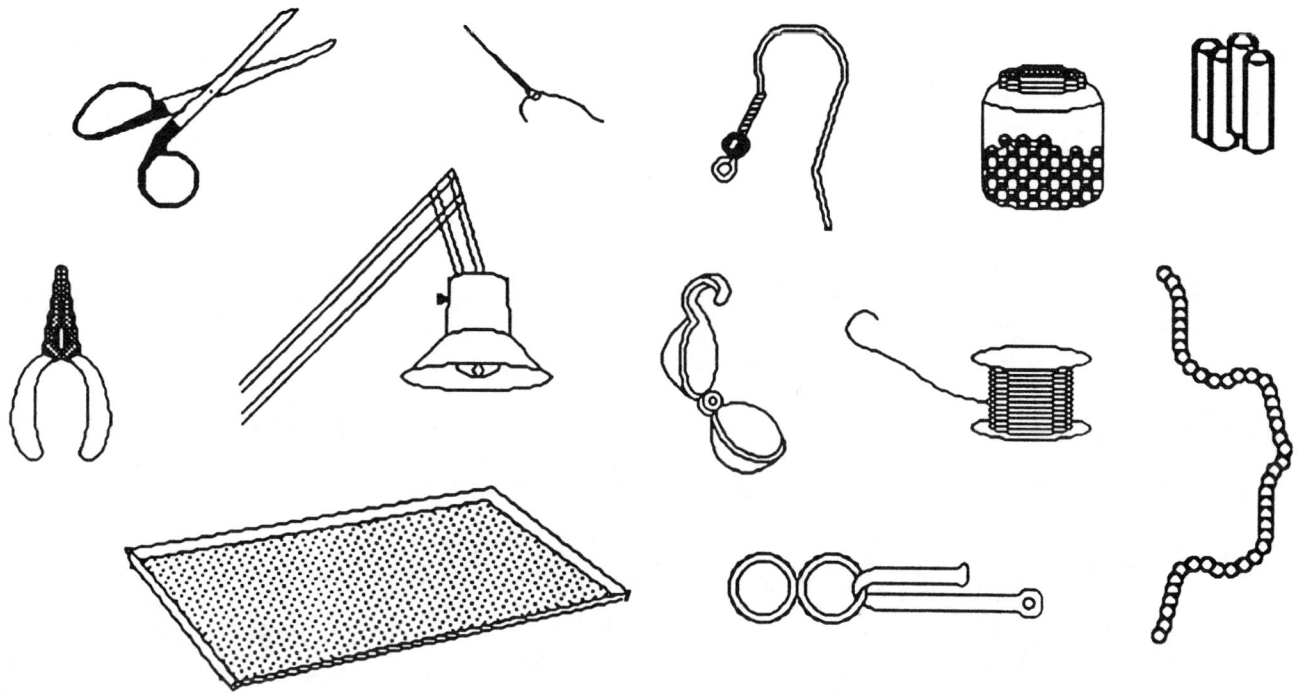

BASIC
BEADING

SUPPLIES

BEADS

Beads come in a variety of shapes, colors, and sizes. Sizes can range from 8° to 25° (° is pronounced "aught"). The larger the number, the smaller the bead size. In this age of technology you can get any color or hue of the spectrum, especially in the smaller sizes. This can be useful in larger projects or where you would like the color change to be subtle. Smaller beads allow you to go into more detail in your designs.

Beads come in various types and shapes. Bugle beads are cylindrical in shape and range from 3/8 of an inch long to 2 inches. These beads are very useful for brick-laying stitches, fringes, and a variety of other stitches. Seed beads come in many different varieties. As the name implies they are round like most seeds and some are actually made by drilling a hole through a seed. Nowadays, they are made of many different materials, but usually out of glass. These are just two of the more common types of bead.

I make sure I buy enough beads to finish the project that I am working on. Just like yarn and thread, the dye lots change to varying degrees and the shade of blue I bought one week may not be the same the next time I go. How many is enough? When I buy beads, I buy two or three hanks of the same color. A hank has 8 to 12 strands on it. A strand is a single string of beads, 12 to 24 inches long. The number of beads per inch on a strand will vary depending on the size of the beads. I never buy beads in tubes if I can help it. Tubes cost more and have fewer beads than a full hank. If I do run short of a color, I string up the color I need and take it with me when I make the rounds to the different bead shops. Sometimes I get lucky.

BEADS (cont.)

Thrift shops and garage sales are also great places to find beads. I have found lots of good antique beads that way. I've also found that beaders often hoard their beads bringing them out only after much coaxing.

THREAD

Thread comes in a variety of sizes and waxed or unwaxed. Waxed thread is recommended because it makes working the beads easier. You can buy beeswax and a beeswax holder and wax the thread yourself, but buying the thread already waxed is easier and cheaper in the long run.

Thread comes in sizes: AAA, AA, A, B, C, D, E, F, FF, G. The higher the letter in the alphabet, the thicker the thread. Triple A is very thin. It is good for use on the smaller beads. Size G is real thick, good for use on the larger beads. Sometimes you want a thinner thread because of the number of times the thread must pass through the beads.

NEEDLES

Beading needles come in sizes 10 through 16. The larger the number the thinner the needle. These are the gauges I always work with. Companies gauge their needles differently, so when I buy my beads I actually pass the needle through a bead to make sure it will work.

The best way I have found to thread the thinner needles is to cut the thread at an angle, then wet the angled thread and the eye of the needle. Use very good light. The best time to thread needles is during the day when the sun is out. Thread all your needles at the same time and stick them in a pin cushion to use later on.

FINDINGS

What are findings? They are: bead tips, barrel clasps, hook and eye clasps, spring-ring, jump-ring clasps, and earring hooks. These are attached to your work so that it can be worn.

To attach a clasp to my work, I will usually attach a bead tip to my piece first. The clasp can be added to the bead tip later with a pair of pliers. To attach a bead tip to your piece, position the needle in the main body where you want the clasp to go. Pick up a bead on the needle and pass the needle through the bottom of the bead tip (the hook should be on top). Pick up another bead. Pass the needle through the top of the bead tip, down through the bead and into the main body of the piece. Remember, this is where your piece will take the most stress, so pass the needle back and forth a few times.

Findings can be found in most any bead shop where you buy your beads. Try to get bead tips and attach your clasps to them. It looks more professional that way. Add a drop of jeweler's glue to the bead resting inside the bead tip for extra holding strength.

BASIC TECHNIQUES

THREAD TENSION

Thread tension is something that should be discussed. This is how hard you pull on the thread after passing the needle through a bead that is already attached to the piece you are working on. It can be very frustrating to a new bead artist. The only way to learn it is by trial and error. Most likely, your first piece won't look like you want it to because it is either too tight or too loose. Stick with it. Thread tension is something that is developed over time and requires patience. Just keep at it. Remember, the tension for each piece is different.

STARTING and FINISHING

In the first edition of this book I recommended burning the tail end of the thread. Some of my beading buddies objected to it, disagreeing with the concept. Burning thread ends is an art, so for a beginning bead artist this would be a hard accomplishment. So we won't do that any more.

Here is a simpler if more tedious way to start:

1. Pick up a bead on the needle. Bring the bead down the thread, leaving 6-8 inches of thread as a tail. Bring the needle up through the bottom or tail end of the bead. When doing this, **DO NOT** split the thread as it will be removed later. It is important not to split the thread unless needed, anyway. Continue with the stitch.

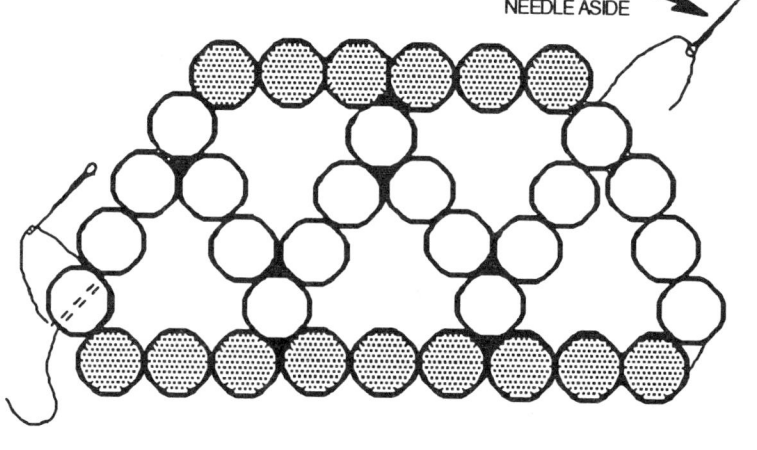

PUT THIS
NEEDLE ASIDE

2. When you are an inch or so into the piece, take a needle and pull on the outer thread of your anchor bead. The thread should slip right out. If not, keep practicing and complete the next step as you would if the thread had slipped out easily.

3. Thread the tail end onto a smaller needle than you were using when you started.

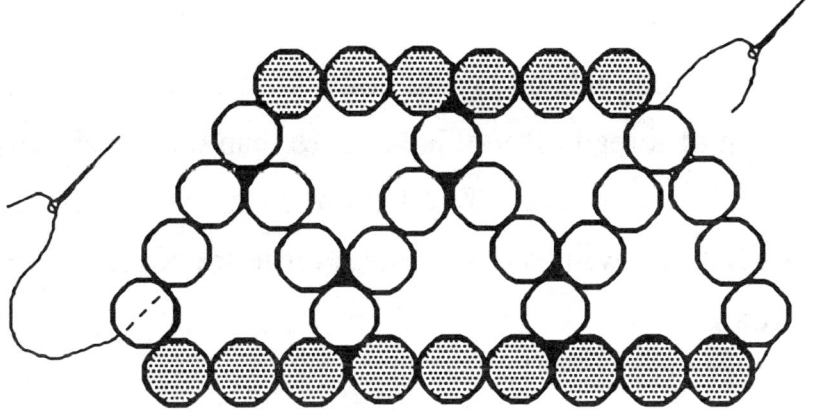

4. Pass the needle back through the piece through one or more beads at a time, and then change directions so that the thread zig-zags back up the piece. Complete this action five or six times, then cut the thread close to the bead it is emerging from.

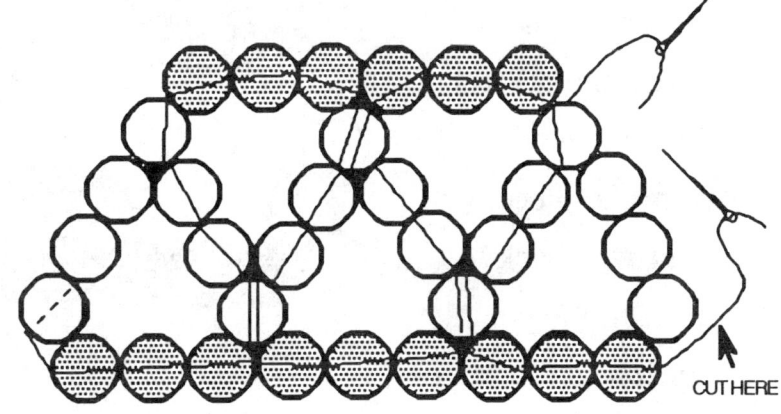

Finishing your piece should be done exactly the same way. Zig-zag the leftover thread back into the finished piece as shown above.

This is really the best method of starting and finishing because there are no unsightly burned ends or knots and the piece can find its own natural tension since there are no balls or knots pulling on the first and last beads.

This method is handy for another problem which often arises, which is running out of thread before you are finished with the piece.

ADDING a NEW THREAD

Stop beading when you get down to about six inches of thread. Cut another
length of thread. If you have more than one needle, use a second needle with the
new piece of thread. If you are down to your last needle you can use the same
one but you will have to rethread it more often. Here is how to work in a new
thread:

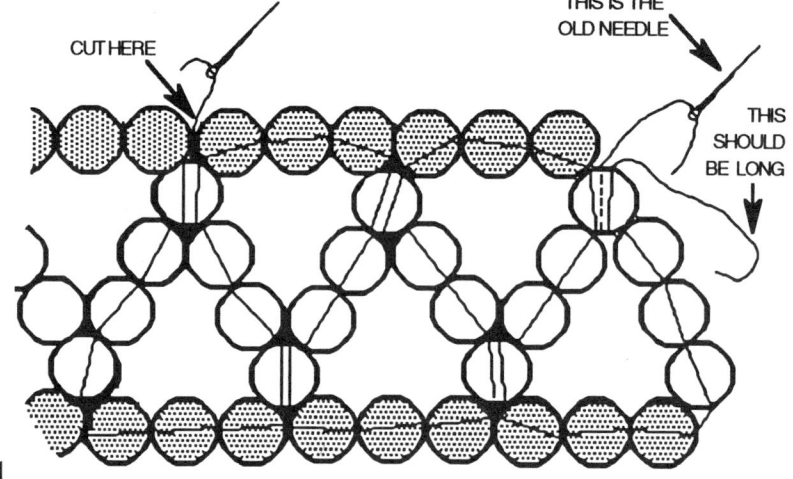

1.   Starting at the point
      where the current
      thread is emerging
      from the piece, work
      your way back
      through the completed
      portion of the piece
      using the zig-zag method described on the previous pages.
      Be sure to leave a long tail as it will become the new thread.

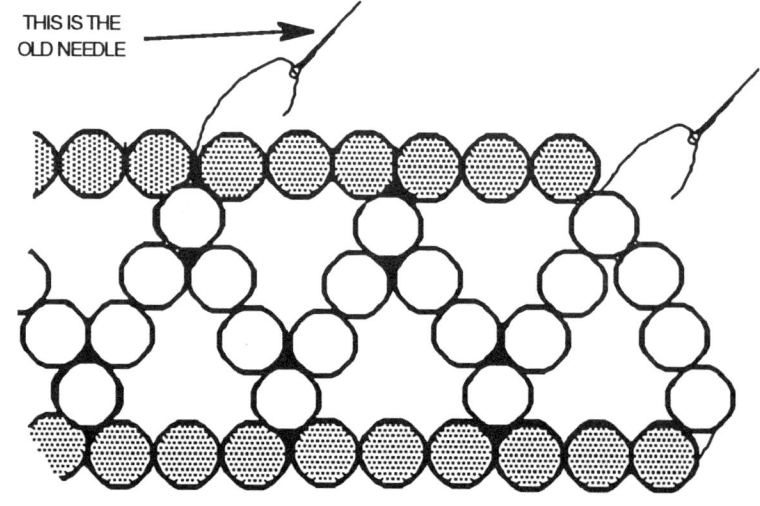

2.   Continue working the
      stitch with the new
      thread. Work an inch
      or so, then pick up the
      old needle and thread.

3.   Now work in a zig-zag fashion through the new portion of the work as described above. This also helps strengthen your piece.

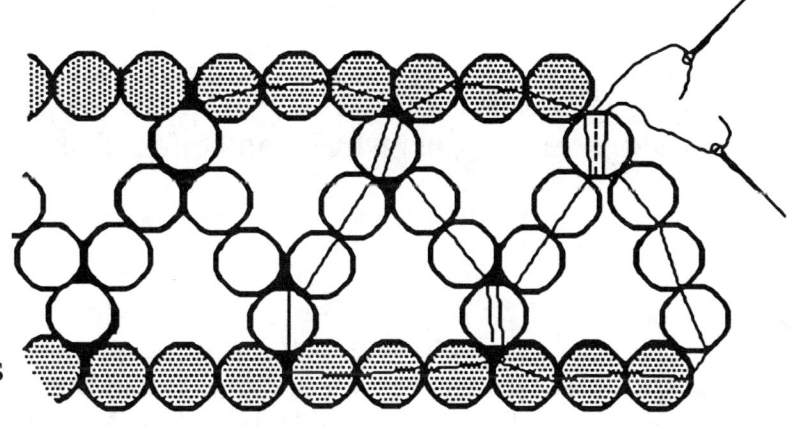

Now, cut the old thread as close to the bead as possible.

You are now ready to continue working on the stitch from where you left off. It may seem easier to work the short thread up through the piece and cut it off before you work the new thread in, especially if you only have one needle, but don't be tempted to do it this way because then it is very difficult to find that last bead (where you stopped) with the new thread since the old thread has already been concealed.

ENVIRONMENT

Good light in your work area is extremely important.   I can't stress this enough; daylight hours are best. During the dark hours use a very good light. Magnifying lamps work quite well when you are beading at night.

Last but not least, remember to take frequent breaks when you are working with your beads. Stretch, take a walk and look at the scenery. Otherwise you'll get cramped up, and it won't be fun any more.

Above all, *HAVE FUN WITH IT !*

OTHER SUPPLIES

SUPER-GLUE

This is useful in securing bead tips (see Findings). It should be used as sparingly as possible. Do NOT use Krazy-Glue as it is too runny. A good jeweler's glue, which can be found at most craft stores, is best.

GRAPH PAPER

Use graph paper to work out some of your more complicated designs, especially fringe. My theory is if it can be drawn, it can be done in beadwork. Scientific graph paper works very well for this.

COLORED PENCILS

These are useful with graph paper for working out designs. Try to get a wide range of colors.

SMALL JARS and CONTAINERS

Useful for holding beads, thread, findings, and needles.

DOUBLE-STICK TAPE

Can be purchased in any five and dime store, or craft store. It is useful for holding your work to the table when you are doing fringe work.

SMALL TRAY

Line the tray with velours or velvet to help avoid chasing runaway beads.

NEEDLE-NOSE PLIERS

These are very handy to have around for attaching findings. They can reach into a piece and grab a very short thread end. Although I don't recommend it, they can also be used to break a bead for removal from a piece.

OTHER SUPPLIES (cont.)

SCISSORS

These should be small and sharp. Manicure scissors work very well.

TWEEZERS

These are optional. I don't use them myself but I have small slender hands.
You may find them handy for picking up beads.

NEEDLE THREADER

This item works fine for the larger needles but is pretty useless for the
smaller ones. It is not really necessary.

MAGNIFYING DESK LAMP

This is a nice item to have if its possible. Get the kind that mount on the
side of the table and have an adjustable arm if you can.

CHAPTER 2

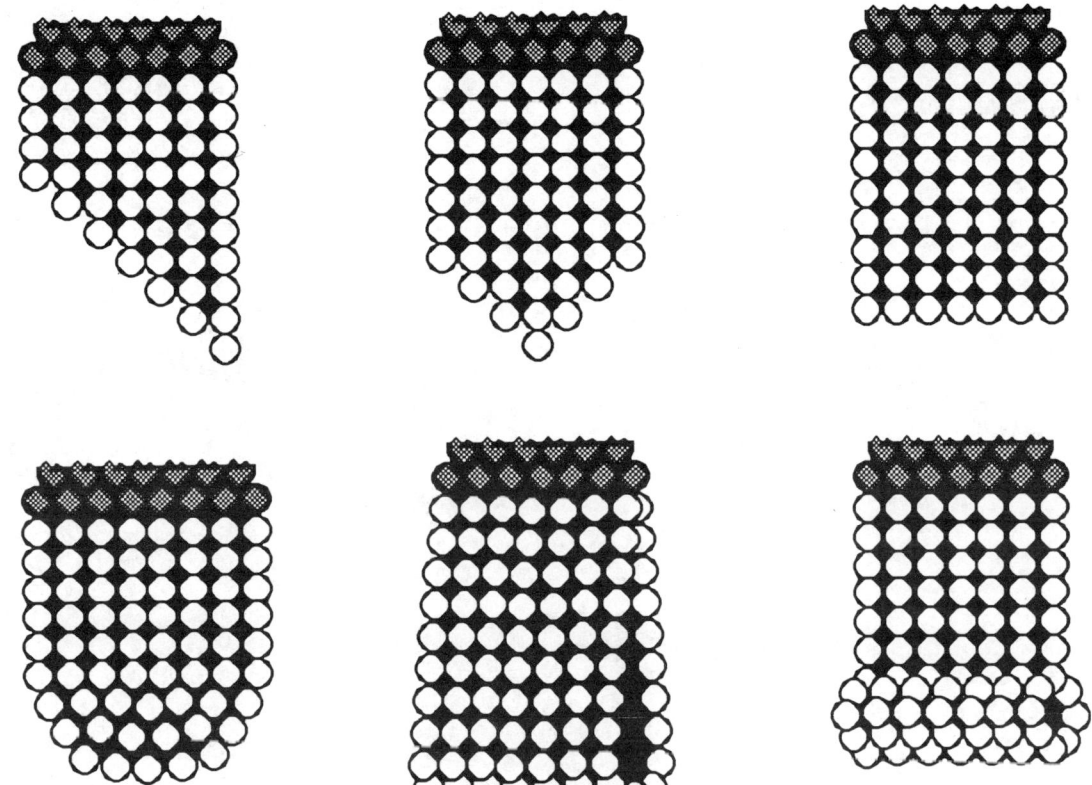

BEADWORK
FRINGES

FRINGE

Fringe can be the most important part of your piece. It can make or break it. The use of graph paper can be helpful in visualizing and laying out your design ideas.

The fringe can consist of seed beads and/or bugle beads. The use of bugle beads can be a real eye-catcher in earrings and neck-chest pieces. The fringe is an integral part of the Commanche stitch. The use of porcupine quills can be very eye-catching.

DESIGN

Let's talk a little about designing the fringe and how to work it so that it looks like what you have on graph paper. Sometimes that doesn't happen because when you buy a hank of beads, you will often get some misshapen beads in with the good ones. Therefore, before you start, make sure you remove all the warped and misshapen beads so that all of your beads are the same size.

Use colored pencils to help you visualize the colors in your design. Anything can be accomplished with careful planning and plotting on paper in advance.

BASIC TECHNIQUES

Use the zig-zag method described in Chapter One to attach the threads which will be used for fringe. Work your way down to the outer edge bead where the fringe will start. This outer edge bead can be either a seed bead or a bugle bead.

I usually anchor my piece to the surface of the work table with double-stick tape, leaving enough room to work the fringe comfortably. If I am adding fringe to an earring, I just hold it in my hand.

Pick up the beads on the needle just as you have the design laid out on paper. Watch carefully as you progress. It is very easy to skip a strand or repeat one if you are not alert.

BASIC TECHNIQUES
(Continued)

On a small piece I use only one thread and needle. For larger pieces, I always anchor the piece with tape (see pg. 11) and use multiple threads and needles, one coming from each bead that will have a fringe strand attached. But what to do with all those threads? I start near the top of the main piece and work my way down with as many zig-zags as possible for each thread. I never pass the needle straight down through the piece as this puts more stress on the fringe thread and is likely to pull right out. I always end in the same manner, working toward the top of the piece. I use scissors that are small and sharp. This allows me to cut the thread very close to the bead it is emerging from. I do this by folding the piece where I end so that the top of the bead is exposed. Then I cut the thread as close to the bead as possible without cutting the other threads.

Here are a few of the fringe effects that I have used over the years. In the following examples, the main body of the piece is represented with darker colored beads.

U-SHAPED LOOP

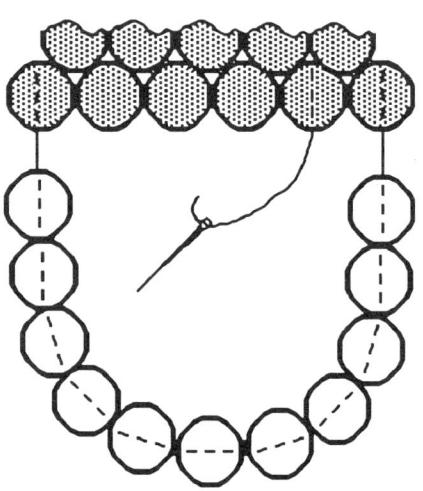

For this fringe an even number of beads on the outer edge of the main body are needed. Attach the thread to the main body of the piece, working your way to the outer edge bead. Pick up the number of beads desired for the outer (and longest) loop. Pass the needle up through the opposite outer edge bead on the main body of the piece. Now pass the needle down through the adjacent outer edge bead (as shown at left) so that it is in position to start the next loop. Continue in this manner until finished with the two center on the outer edge of the main piece. Work the needle back up through the main body of the piece, ending next to the darkest bead.

STRAIGHT FRINGE

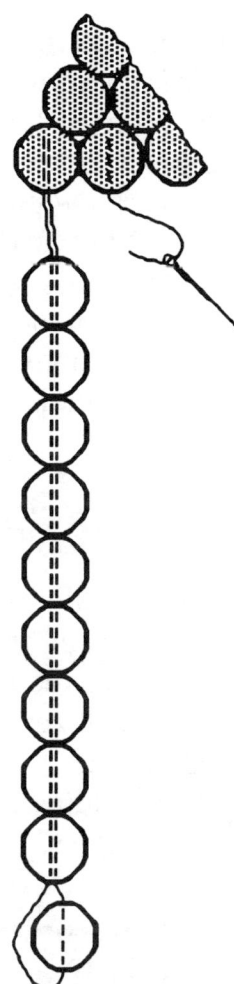

Pick up 30-40 beads with the needle for
a long fringe (less for a shorter one).
Pass the needle back up through all the
beads except for the last one that was
picked up (as shown at right). Now pass
the needle back up through the outer
edge bead of the main body and down
through the next bead so that the needle
is in position to start the next strand.
Keep repeating this process until
finished adding strands. Work the
needle back up through the main body
of the piece, ending next to the darkest
bead.

CIRCLE FRINGE

Attach the thread to the main body of the piece.   Work your way to the outer
edge bead. Pick up the number of beads desired for length. Now pick up 6 to 8
beads (more for a larger circle) and pass the needle back up through the others
(as shown below) and back up through the first outer edge bead so that the needle
is in position for the next strand. Keep repeating this step until finished. Work
the needle back up through the main body of the piece ending next to the darkest
bead.

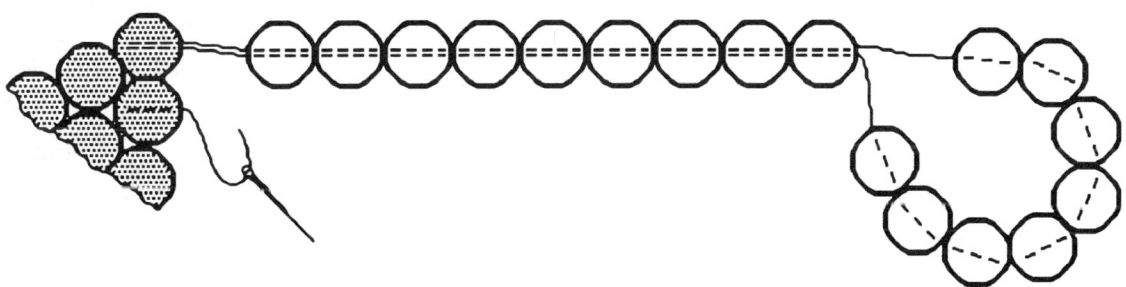

LOOPED FRINGE

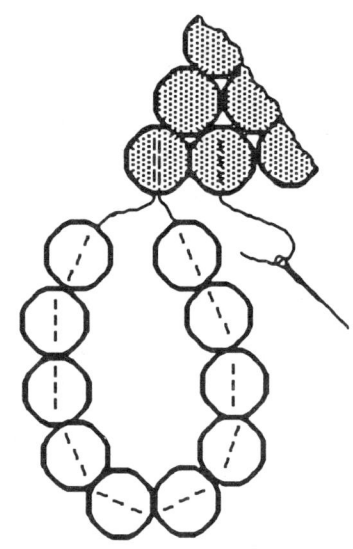

Attach the thread to the main body of the piece
working your way to the outer edge bead. Pick up
the number of beads desired. Pass the needle back
up through the same outer edge bead of the main
body. Now pass the needle down through the next
outer edge bead so that the needle is in position for
the next looped strand. Continue in this manner
until finished. Work the needle back up through
the main body of the piece ending next to the
darkest bead.

GRADUATED FRINGE

This technique can produce a very pleasing effect. Graduated fringe can be
incorporated into all of the styles described in previous sections of this chapter
with the exception of the U-shaped fringe. To create a graduated fringe, one
extra bead (or more) is added to each strand so that the second strand is slightly
longer than the first. When two or more beads are added at a time, the effect
can be quite dramatic.

To create a V-shaped graduated fringe, an odd number of
beads on the outer edge of the main body of the piece is
necessary. After the middle fringe strand has been
attached, start decreasing the number of beads for each
new strand by the same amount as you were adding to
each new strand up to and including the middle strand.
(Shown on the left).

For a right-angle or left-angle graduated fringe, add or
subtract the extra beads for each consecutive strand but
don't change after the middle strand as in the V-shaped
graduated fringe. For this style, the number of beads on
the outer edge of the main body ofthe piece can be either
even or odd. (Shown on the right).

CHAPTER 3

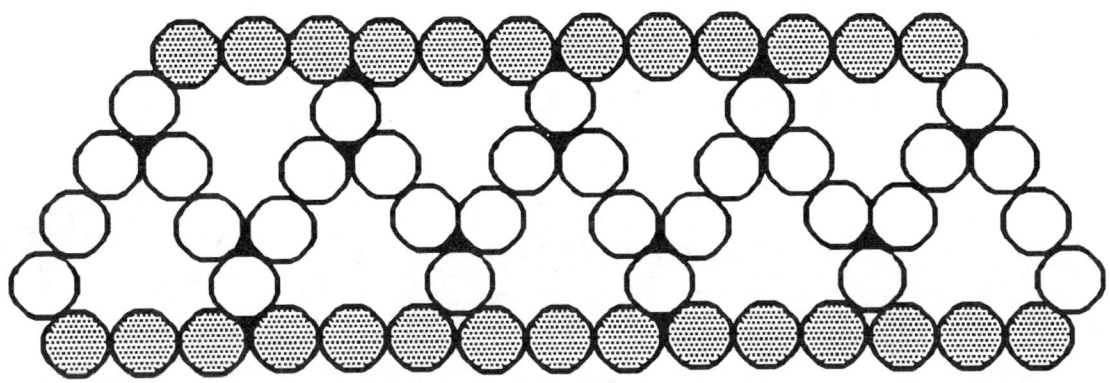

CHEVRON
CHAIN

The Chevron Chain stitch can be used for bracelets, anklets, necklaces and chokers. The tension for this stitch should be moderately tight. Remember that getting the thread tension right is something that must be developed with time and practice. Tension is particularly critical with this stitch so it may take a few attempts before you find the right feel for it. Don't get discouraged if it doesn't come out right at first.

CHEVRON CHAIN

1. Pick up a bead on the needle. Pull the bead down the thread, leaving six to eight inches of thread as a tail. Now pass the needle up through the bottom of the bead. Try not to split the thread as it will be removed later. See Starting and Finishing in Chapter One (pg. 4) for detailed explanations of this process.

2. Pick up six light beads (#2 through #7) and three dark beads (#8 through #10) with the needle.

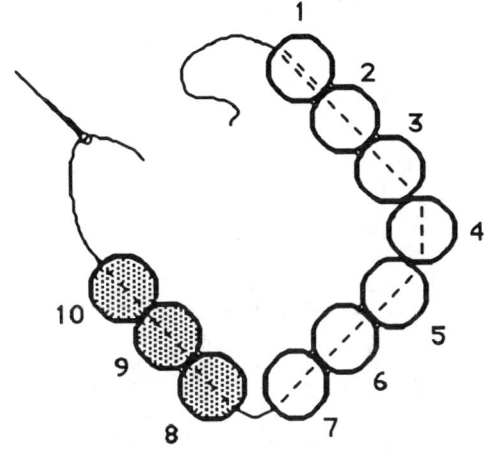

3. Pass the needle through the first four light beads (#1 through #4) a second time and pull the thread tight to form an angle.

4. Pick up three dark beads (#11, #12 and #13), the three light beads (#14, #15 and #16) on the needle.

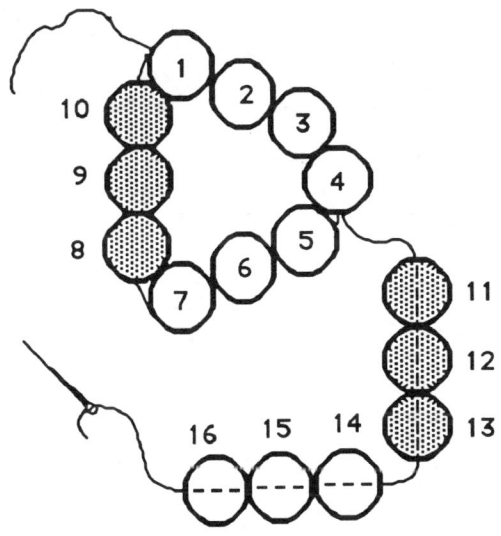

19

CHEVRON CHAIN

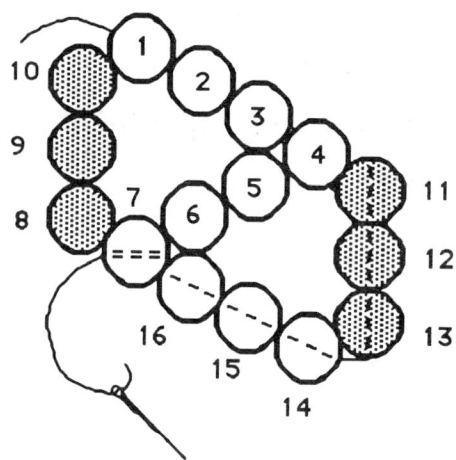

5. Pass the needle through bead #7 and pull the thread tight.

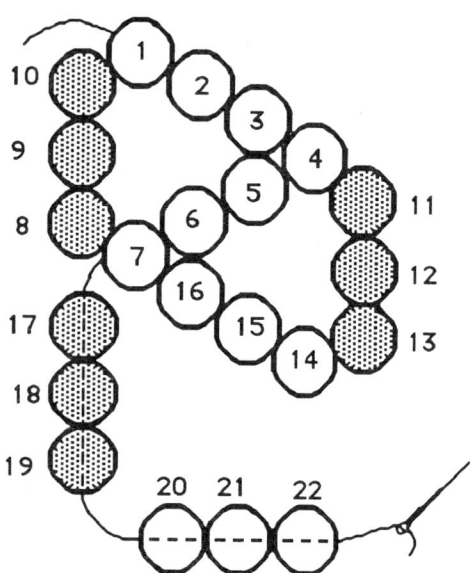

6. Pick up three more dark beads (#17, #18 and #19) and three more light beads (#20, #21 and #22) on the needle.

7. Pass the needle through bead #14 as shown at right and pull the thread tight.

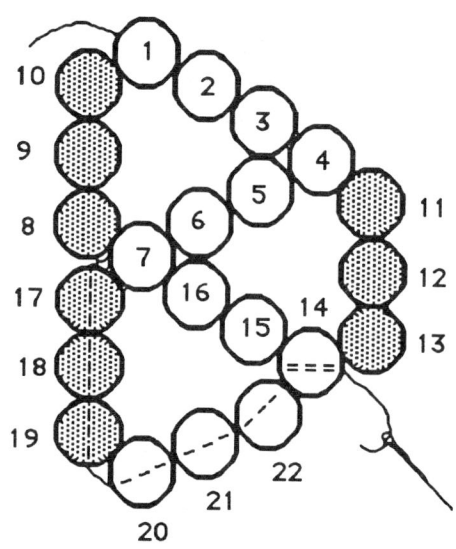

CHEVRON CHAIN

8. Pick up three more dark beads (#23, #24 and #25) and three more light beads (#26, #27 and #28) on the needle.

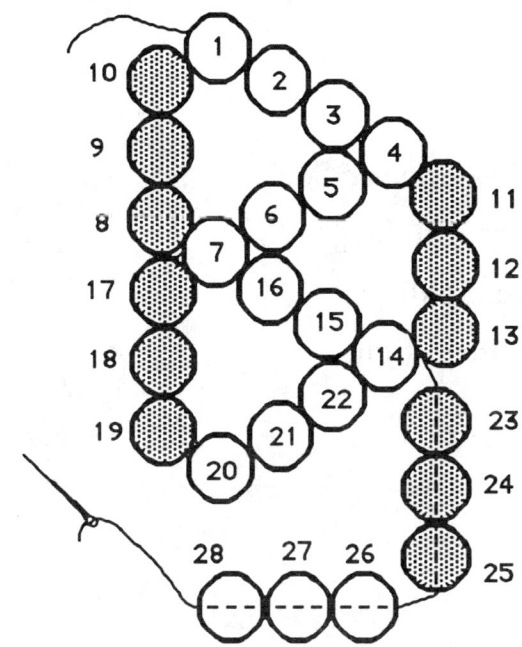

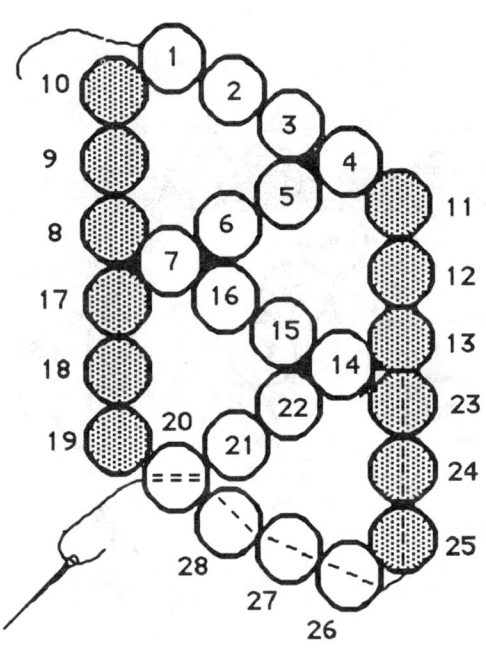

9. Pass the needle through bead #20 and pull the thread tight as shown at left.

10. Pick up three more dark beads (#29, #30 and 31) and three more light beads (#32, #33 and #34) on the needle.

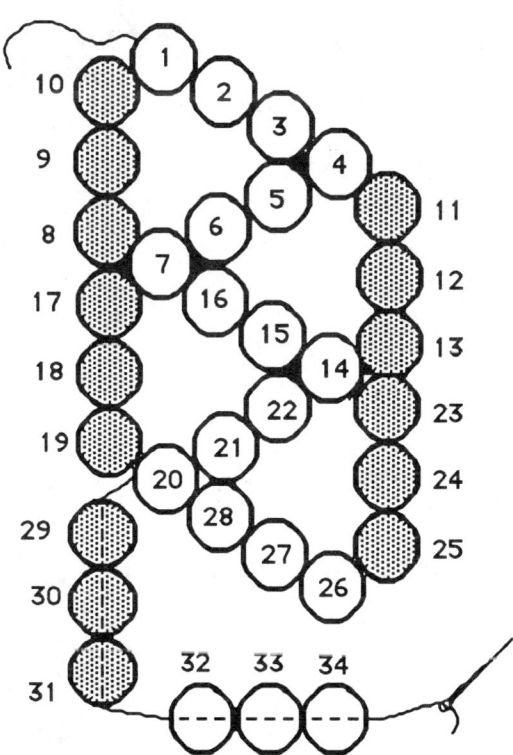

CHEVRON CHAIN

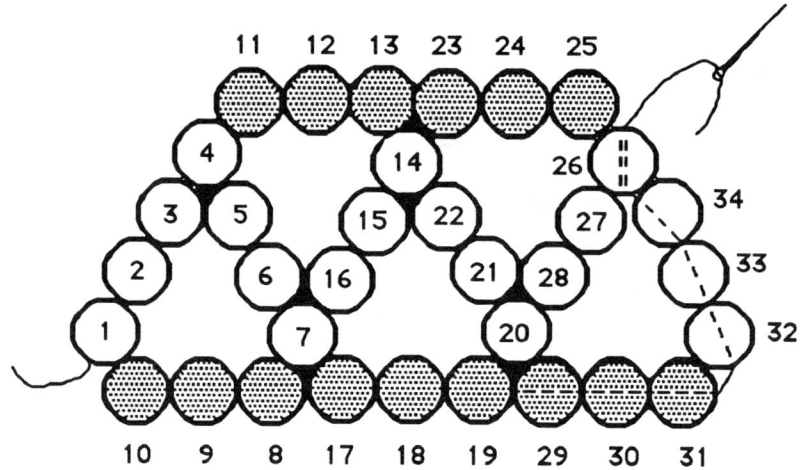

11. Pass the needle through bead #26 and pull the thread tight.

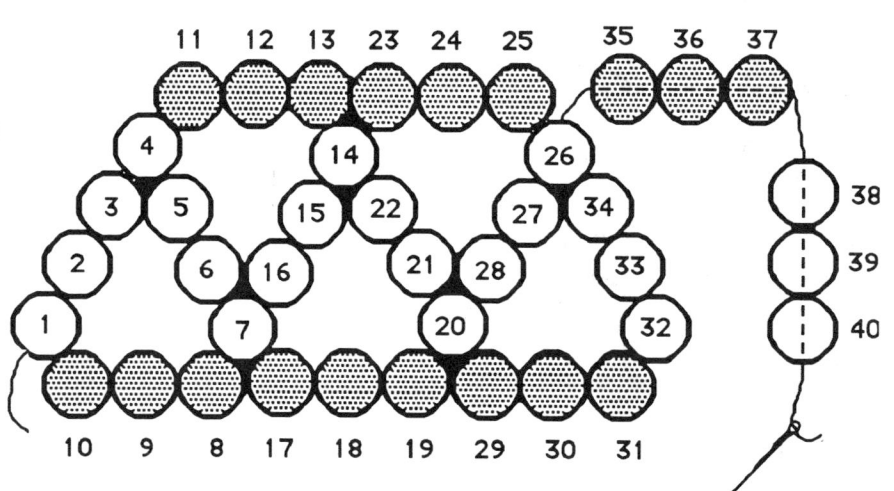

12. Pick up three more dark beads (#35, #36 and #37) and three more light beads (#38, #39 and #40) on the needle.

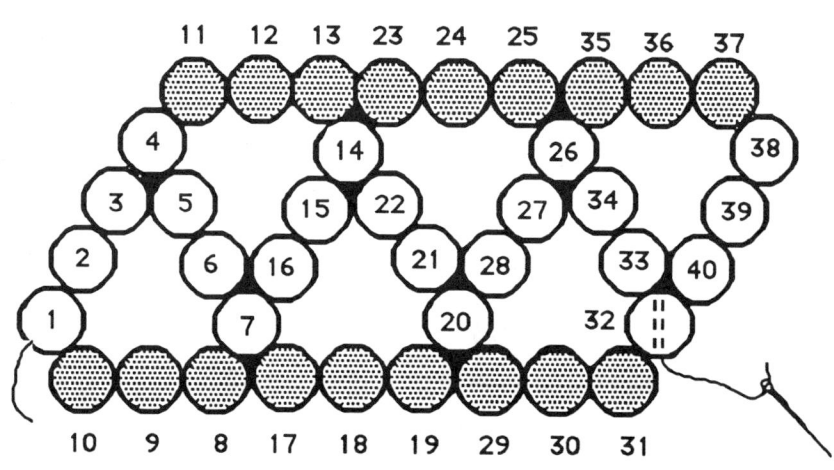

13. Pass the needle through bead #32 and pull the thread tight.

CHEVRON CHAIN

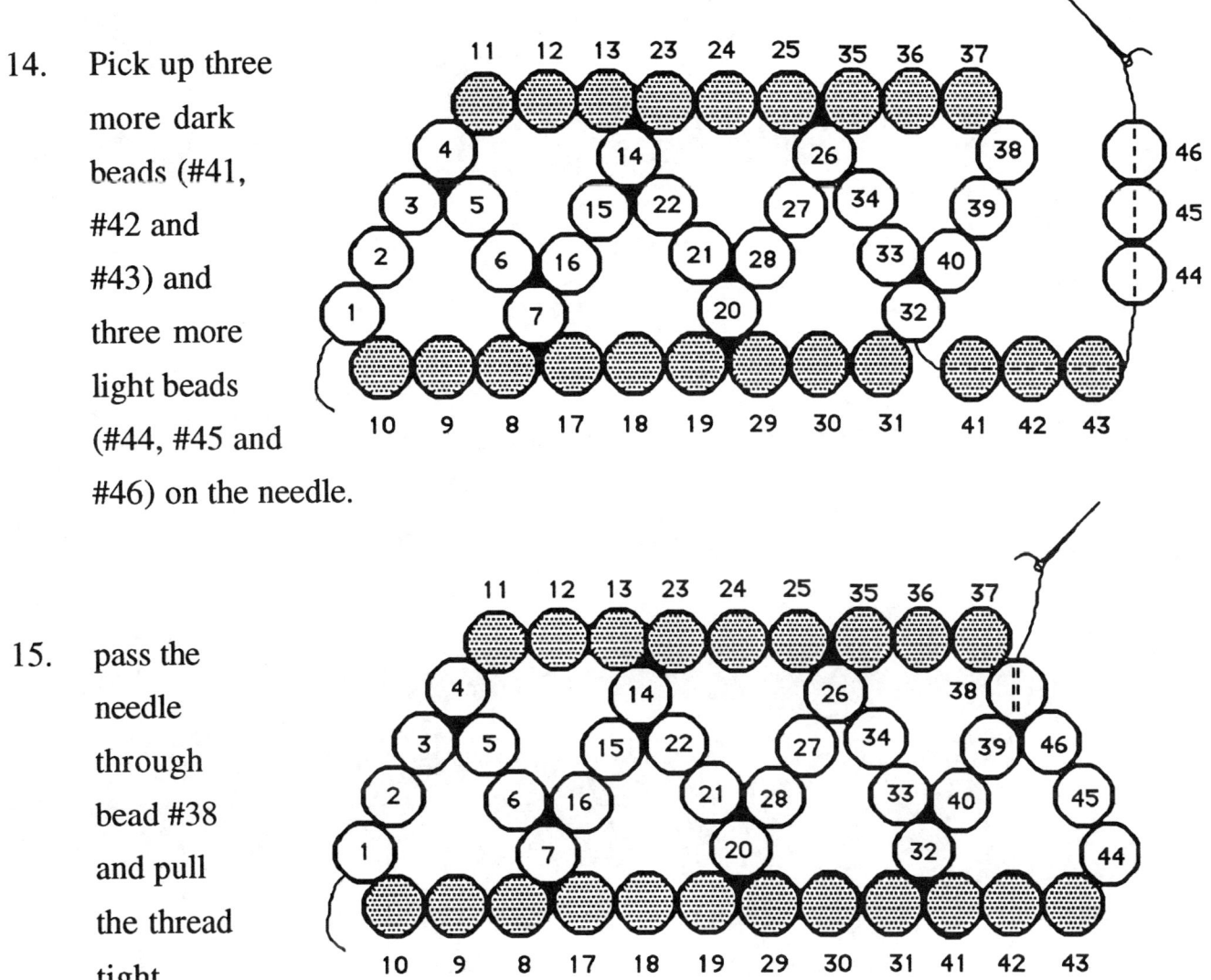

14. Pick up three more dark beads (#41, #42 and #43) and three more light beads (#44, #45 and #46) on the needle.

15. pass the needle through bead #38 and pull the thread tight.

At this point you may want to work the thread tail emerging from bead #1 back into the piece using the zig-zag method described in the Starting and Finishing section of Chapter One (pg. 4).

You may continue in this manner until your chain reaches the desired length. Then cut the thread (if necessary) leaving six to eight inches. Work the tail back into the chain using the zig-zag method. Fringe may now be added to one of the outer edges (consisting of the dark beads). The techniques for adding various types of fringe are shown in Chapter Two (pg. 11).

CHAPTER 4

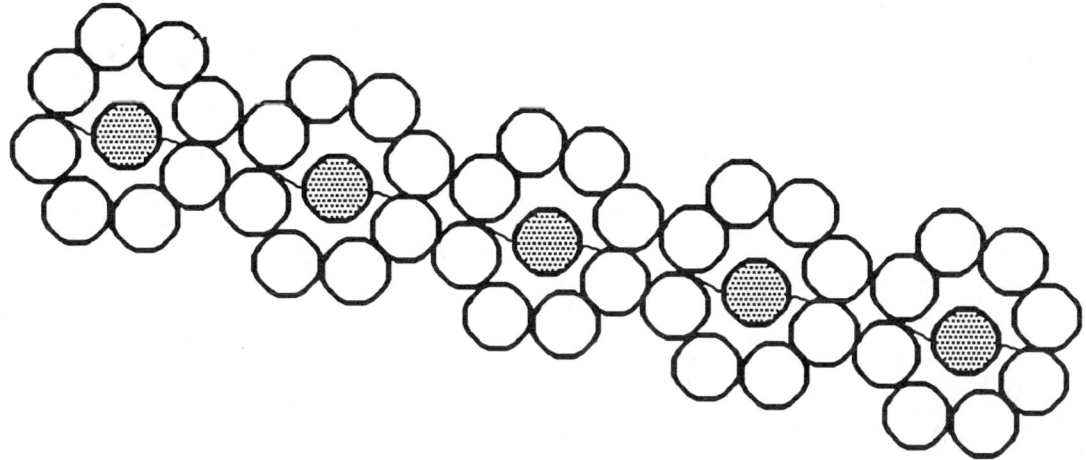

DAISY CHAIN
or
INDIAN FLOWER

The Daisy Chain or Indian Flower stitch is a very pretty one. It can be used for bracelets, anklets, necklaces and chokers. It is a good one to start with if you are a beginner. One possible variation is to use a slightly larger bead size for the center bead of each flower (beads #6 and #15 in the following pages). Try this and watch the effect.

DAISY CHAIN or INDIAN FLOWER

1.   Pick up a light bead on the needle. Pull the bead down the thread, leaving six to eight inches of thread as a tail. Now pass the needle up through the bottom of the bead. Try not to split the thread as it will be removed later. See Starting and Finishing in Chapter One (pg. 4) for detailed explanations of this process.

2.   Pick up four light beads, then one dark bead on the needle. Pass the needle back through bead #1 towards the tail as shown at right.

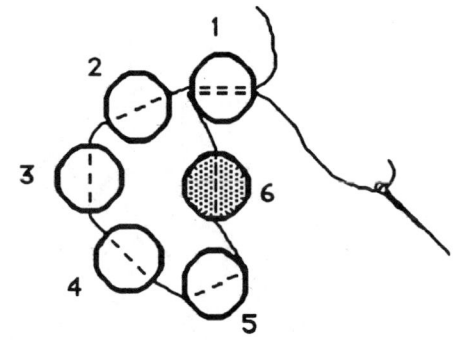

3.   Pick up three more light beads (#7, #8 and #9) and pass the needle through bead #5 as shown at right.

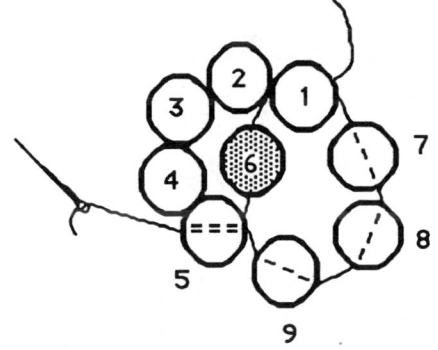

4.   Pick up one light bead (#10) and pass the needle back through bead #9 as shown at right.

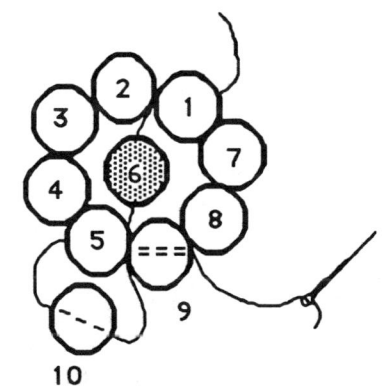

DAISY CHAIN or INDIAN FLOWER

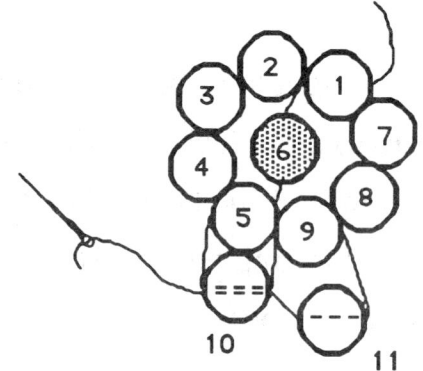

5. Pick up another light bead (#11) and pass the needle back through bead #10.

6. Pick up three more light beads (#12, #13 and #14) and one dark bead (#15). Pass the needle back through bead #11.

7. Pick up three more light beads (#16, #17 and #18) and pass the needle through bead #14.

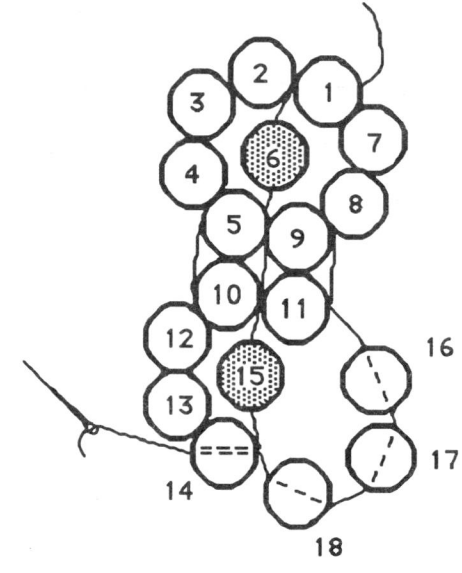

You can keep adding more flowers by repeating steps four through seven. Add nine to all bead numbers each time.

CHAPTER 5

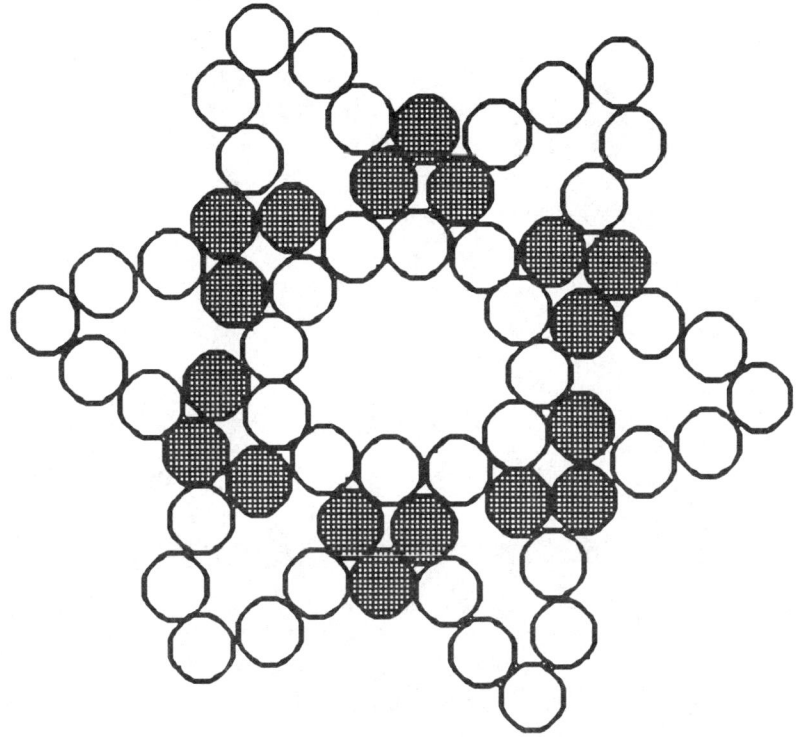

AFRICAN FLOWER MANDALA

The African Flower Mandala stitch can be used for pendants, earrings and even window hangings. This stitch happens to be a favorite of mine because of the many things which can be done with it. Through some experimentation, I've developed other patterns from it which will be available in future editions. After you've done this stitch a few times, try some experimenting of your own.

AFRICAN FLOWER MANDALA

1. Pick up a bead on the needle. Pull the bead down the thread, leaving six to eight inches of thread as a tail. Now pass the needle up through the bottom of the bead. Try not to split the thread as it will be removed later. See Starting and Finishing in Chapter One (pg. 4) for detailed explanations of this process.

Row One or Base

2. String eleven more beads onto the needle and make a circle by passing the needle through bead #1 another time.

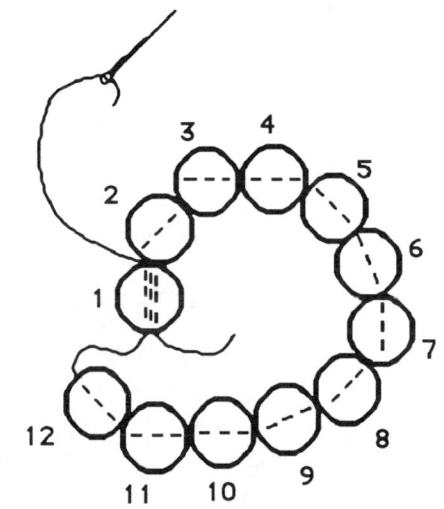

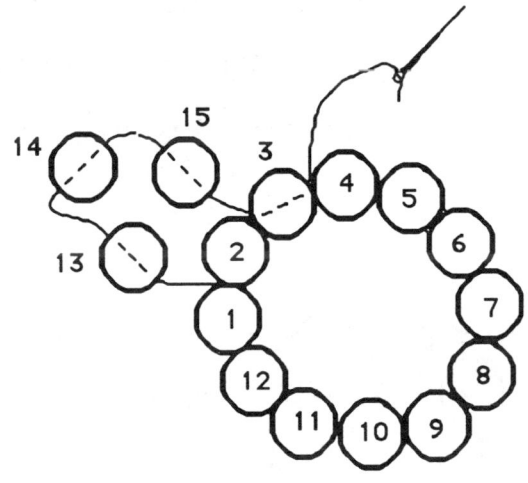

Row Two

3. Pick up three beads (#13, #14 and #15) and pass the needle through bead #3.

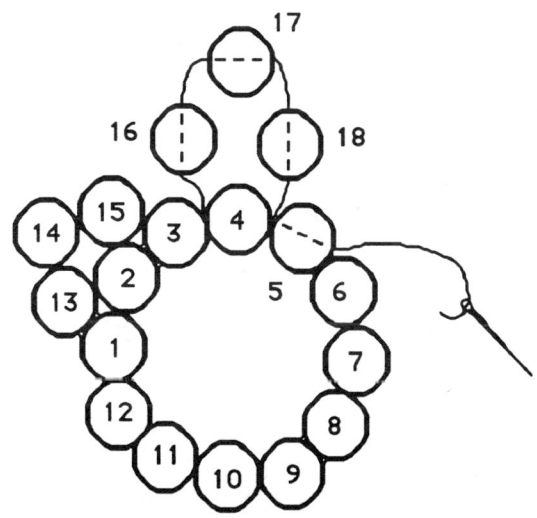

4. Pick up three beads (#16, #17 and #18) and pass the needle through bead #5.

5. Continue in this manner (picking up three more beads each time) for beads #7, #9, #11 and #1 as shown at the right.

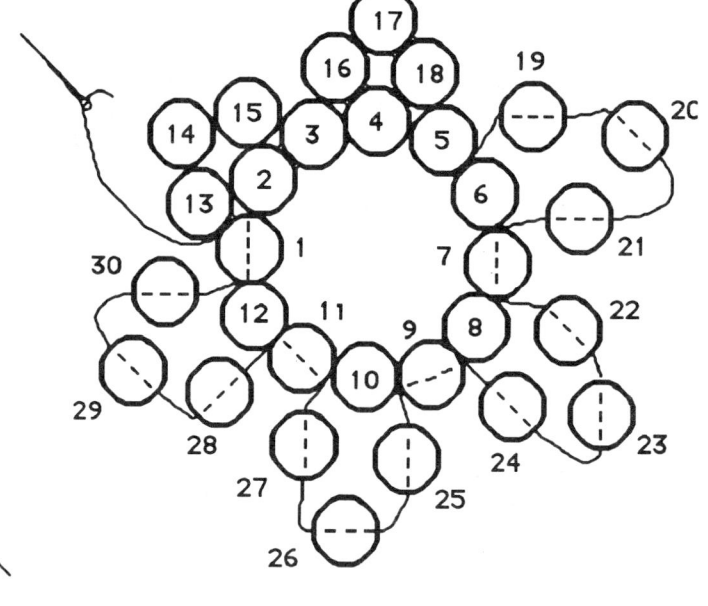

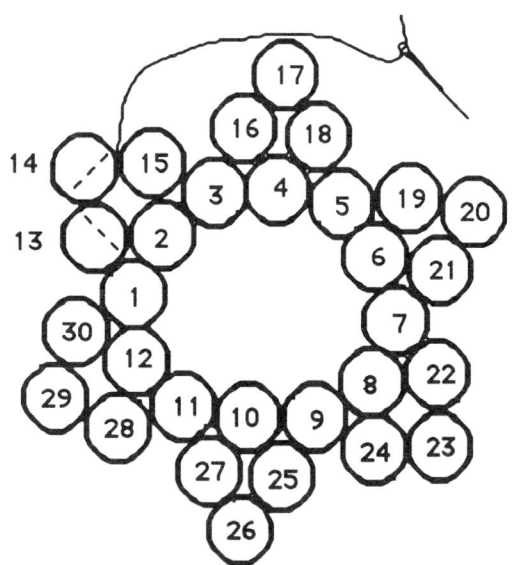

6. Now pass the needle back through beads #13 and #14 as shown at the left.

Row Three

7. Pick up five beads (#31 through #35) and pass the needle through bead #17.

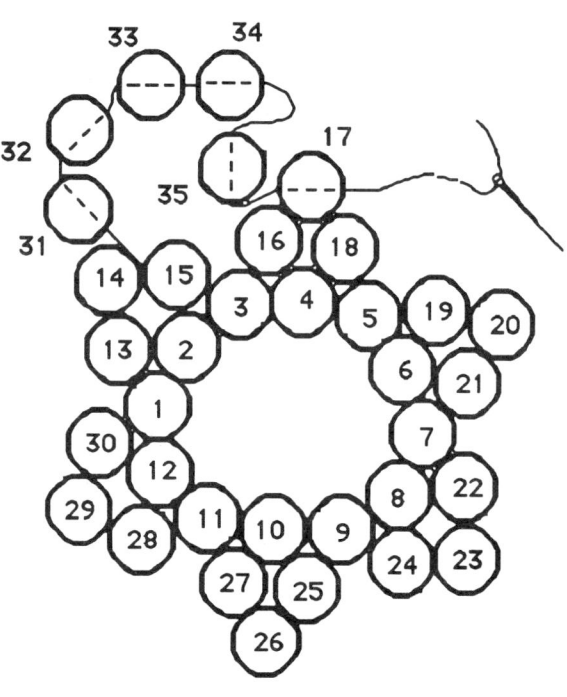

AFRICAN FLOWER MANDALA

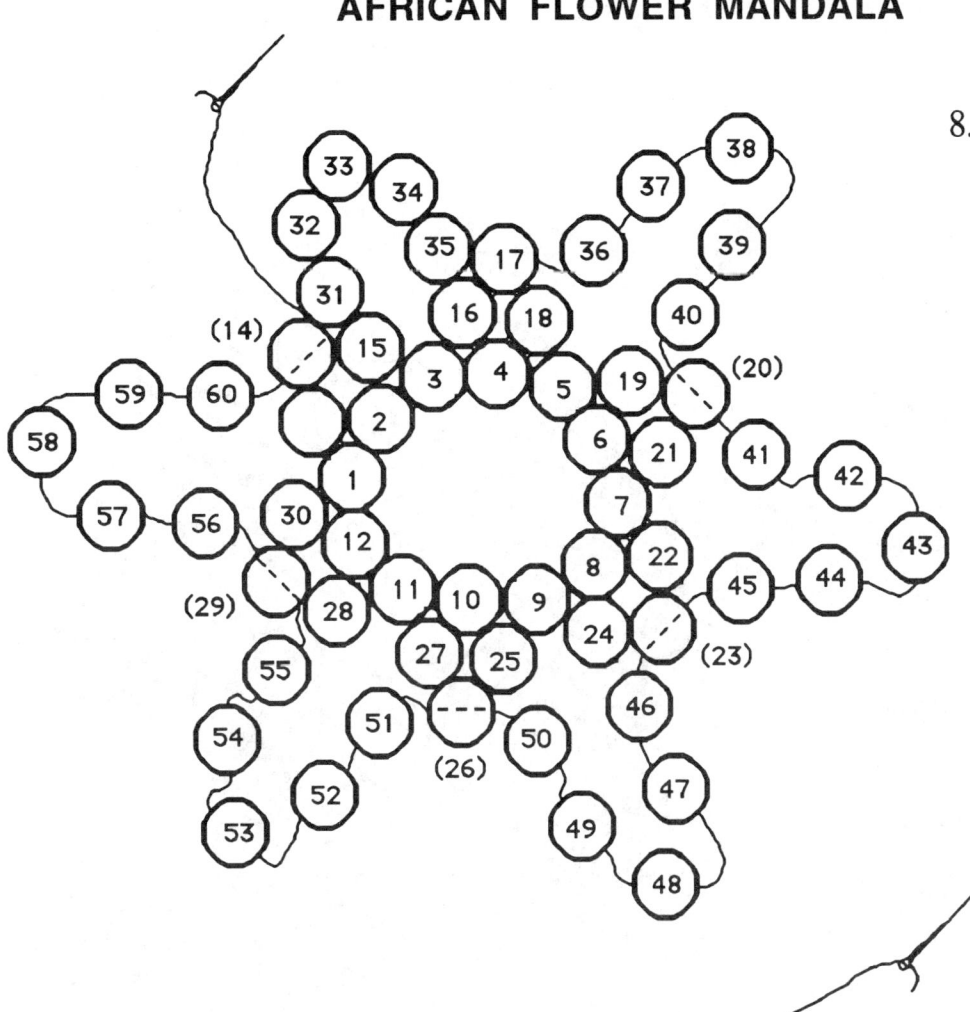

8. Continue in this manner (picking up five beads each time) for beads #20, #23, #26, #29 and #14 as shown at the left. Then pass the needle back through beads #31, #32 and #33 as shown below.

You may stop here or keep adding more rows by adding two to the number of beads in each 'petal' (i.e. there will be seven beads per 'petal' in the next row). Fringe is usually added to the outer row. This is explained in Chapter Two (pg. 11).

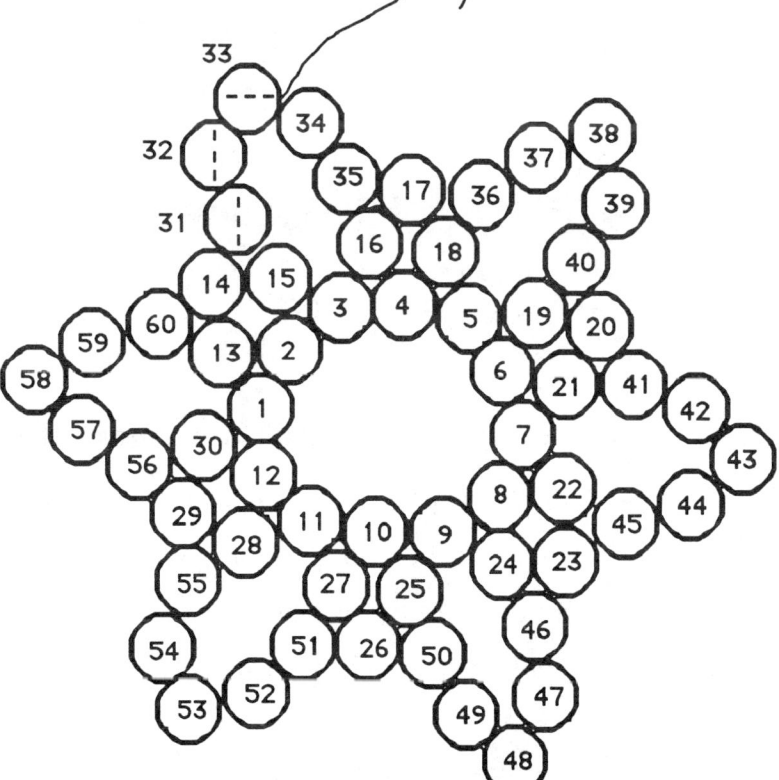

AFRICAN FLOWER MANDALA

You may wish to attach an earwire to this piece. If so, pick one of the points (or 'petals'). Work your needle to the middle bead of that 'petal'. Pick up six to eight beads and pass the needle through the same middle bead going in the same direction as the first time.

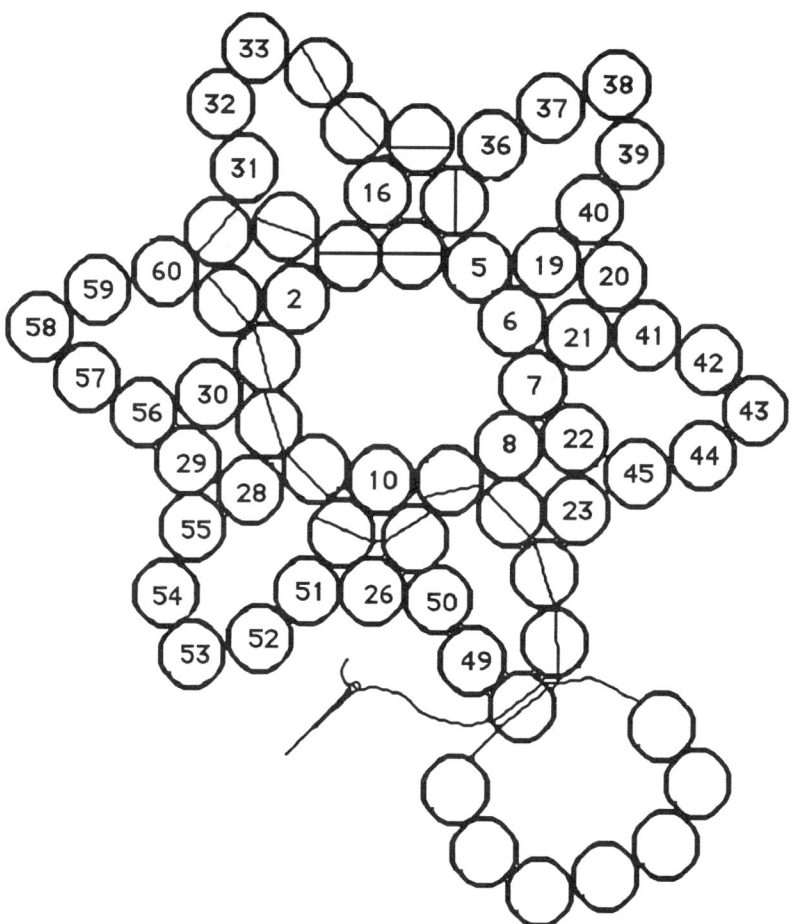

This stitch can also work as a pendant hanging. It is very versatile. You can change the number of 'petals' by changing the number of beads in the first row. The example shown in this chapter has twelve beads in the first row and six 'petals'. Just divide the number of beads in the first row by two to get the number of 'petals' you will end up with.

AFRICAN FLOWER MANDALA

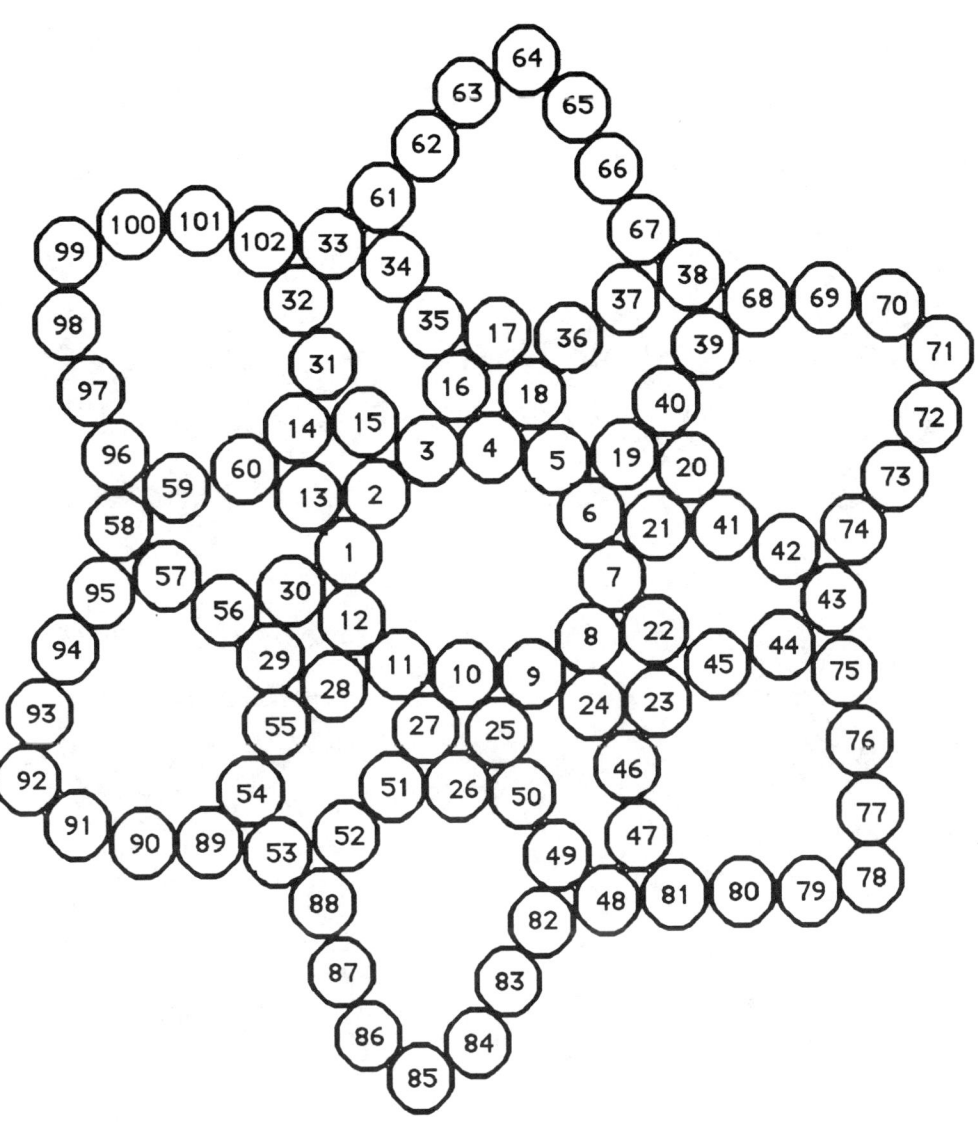

NOTE: A fourth row (seven beads per 'petal')
has been added to the pattern.

Copy this page and use colored pencils to create your own designs.

May be copied for personal use only - ©1990 - In Touch Publishing

AFRICAN FLOWER MANDALA

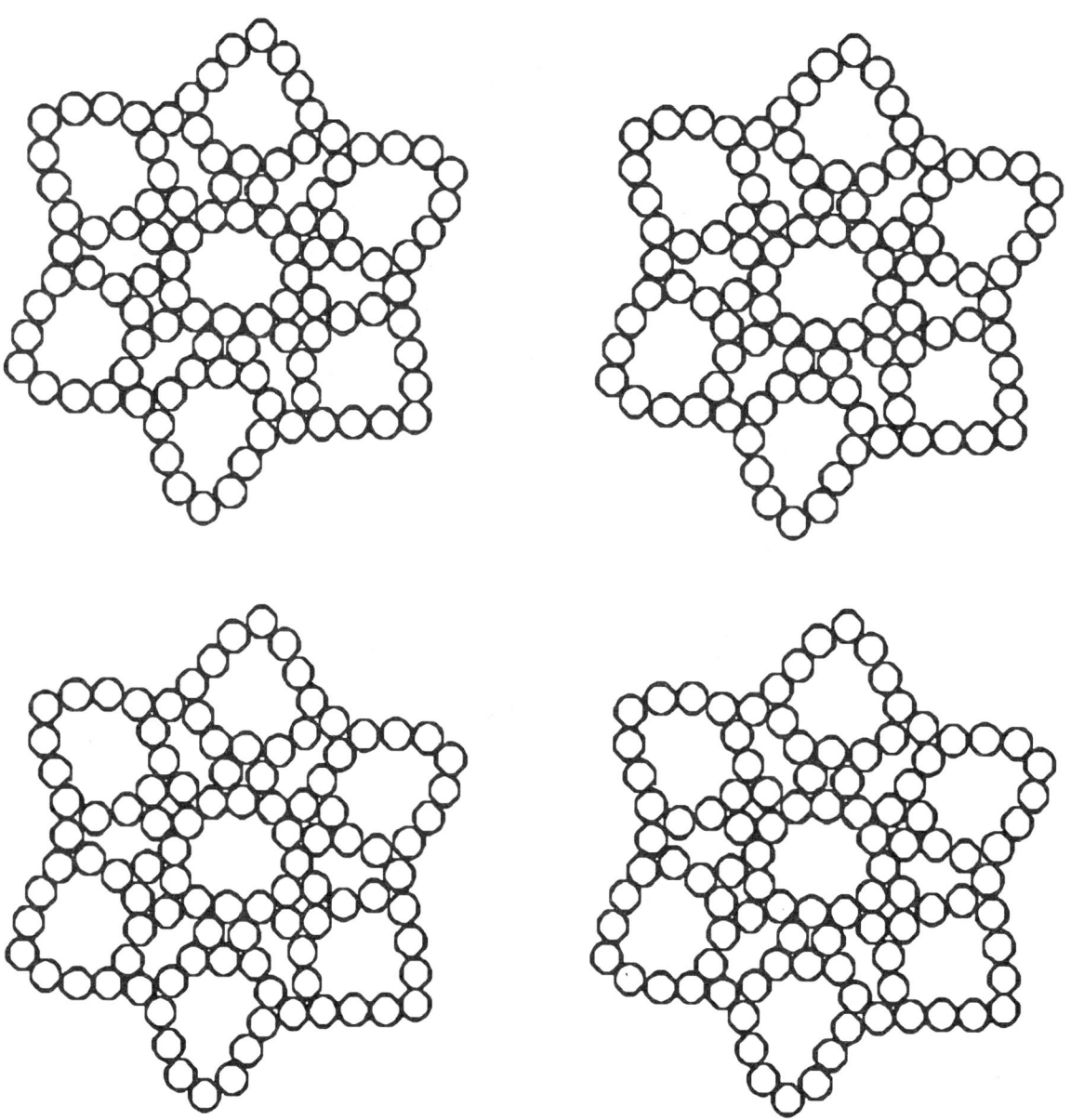

NOTE: A fourth row (seven beads per 'petal')
has been added to the pattern.

Copy this page and use colored pencils to create your own designs.

36

CHAPTER 6

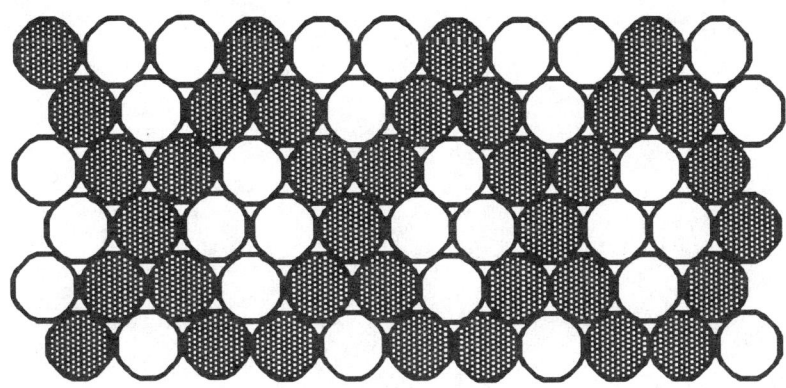

FLAT PEYOTE
OR
TWILL STITCH
(EVEN-NUMBERED)

The Flat Peyote stitch makes very nice bracelets, anklets, chokers and belts. Because the pattern is so regular, you can also design and create very beautiful pictures for wall-hangings. The only limitation here is the number of different colors you have available in beads. I believe that if you can imagine it, you can create it with beads. Use the pattern pages at the back of this chapter to develop your design ideas.

37

FLAT PEYOTE or TWILL STITCH

(Even-numbered)

1. Pick up a bead on the needle. Pull the bead down the thread, leaving six to eight inches of thread as a tail. Now pass the needle up through the bottom of the bead. Try not to split the thread as it will be removed later. See Starting and Finishing in Chapter One (pg. 4) for detailed explanations of this process.

<u>Row One or Base</u>

2. String six more beads onto the needle then pass the needle back through bead #5 in the opposite direction.

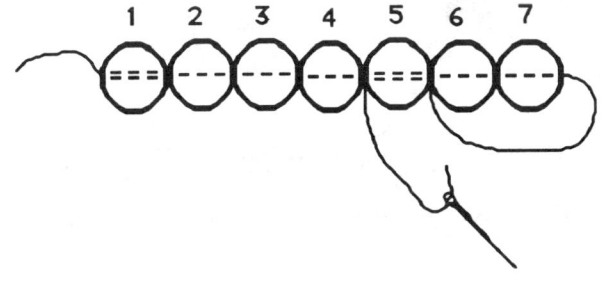

3. Pick up a bead (#8) and pass the needle through bead #3.

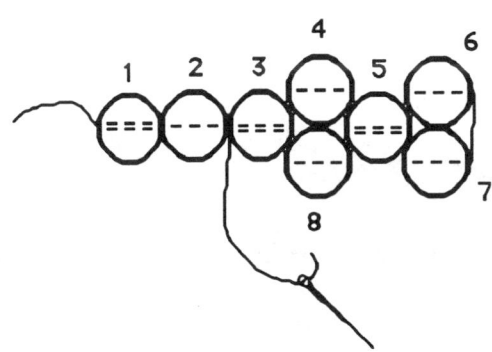

4. Pick up another bead (#9). Pass the needle through bead #1 and pull the thread tight.

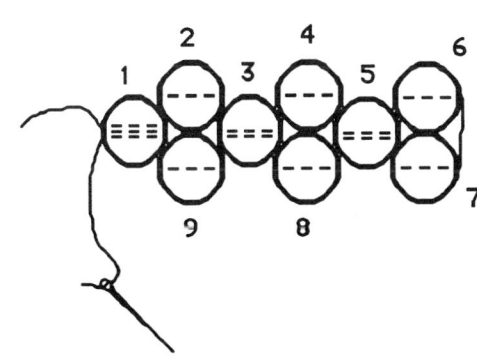

FLAT PEYOTE or TWILL STITCH

(Even-numbered)

<u>Row Two</u>

5.   Pick up a bead (#10) and pass the
      needle back through bead #9.

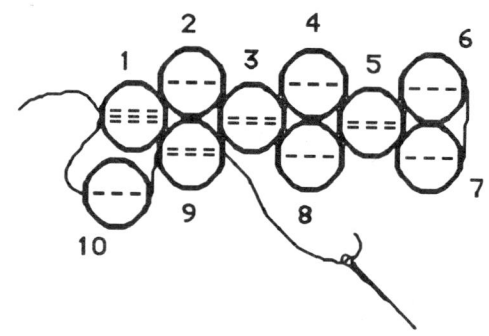

6.   Pick up another bead (#11) and
      pass the needle through bead #8.

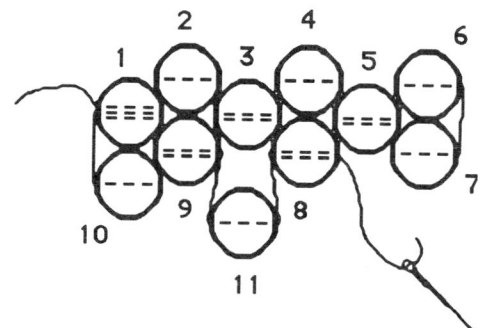

7.   Pick up another bead (#12) and
      pass the needle through bead #7.
      Pull the thread tight.

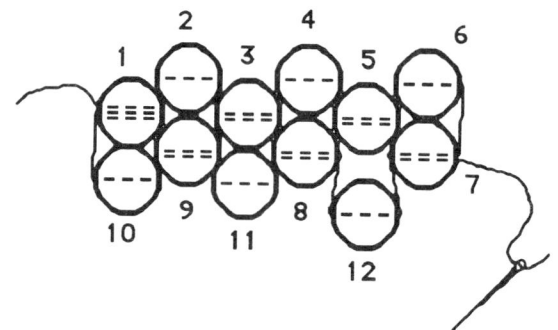

Repeat these steps until the desired length is reached.

FLAT PEYOTE or TWILL STITCH
(Even-numbered)

Copy this page and use colored pencils to create your own designs.

May be copied for personal use only - ©1992 - In Touch Publishing

FLAT PEYOTE or TWILL STITCH
(Even-numbered)

Copy this page and use colored pencils to create your own designs.

FLAT PEYOTE or TWILL STITCH

(Even-numbered)

Copy this page and use colored pencils to create your own designs.

CHAPTER 7

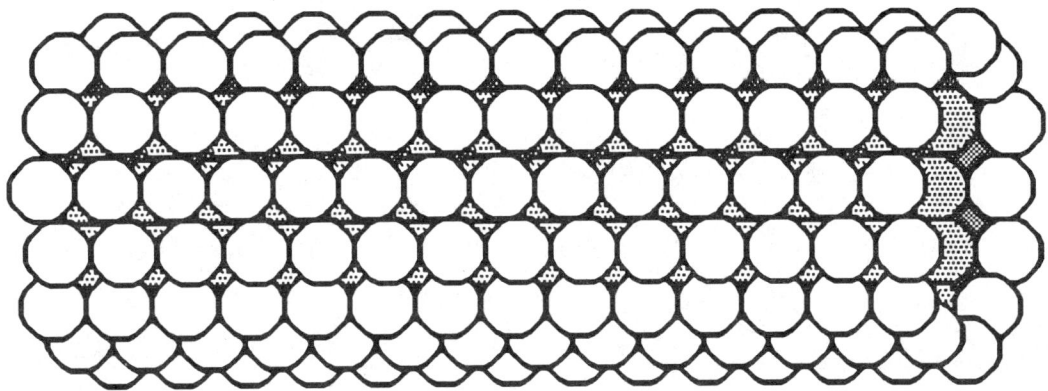

ROUND PEYOTE

(ODD-NUMBERED)

The Round Peyote stitch can be used to make very pretty rope-style bracelets, anklets, necklaces, chokers and belts. Patterns such as daisies, chevrons, lightning bolts, god's eyes and many others can be incorporated into it. Use the pattern page at the end of the chapter to create your own designs. Experiment and have fun with it. You can make very exotic draw-string bag covers. Adding fringe on the bottom can make it even more beautiful. Different types of fringe are explained in Chapter Two (pg. 11). For earrings, do about five to eight rows, then add fringe.

ROUND PEYOTE
(Odd-Numbered)

1. Pick up a bead on the needle. Pull the bead down the thread, leaving six to eight inches of thread as a tail. Now pass the needle up through the bottom of the bead. Try not to split the thread as it will be removed later. See Starting and Finishing in Chapter One (pg. 4) for detailed explanations of this process.

<u>Row One</u>

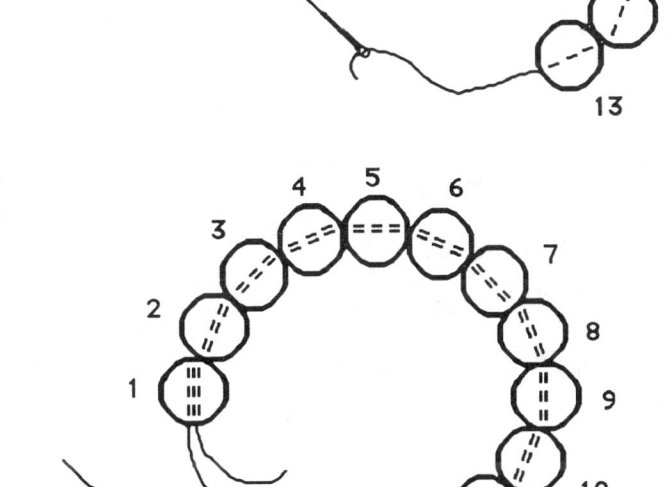

2. String twelve more seed beads onto the needle.

3. Make a circle by passing the needle back through all thirteen beads starting with bead #1.

4. End this first row by passing the needle through bead #1 again. Pull the thread tight.

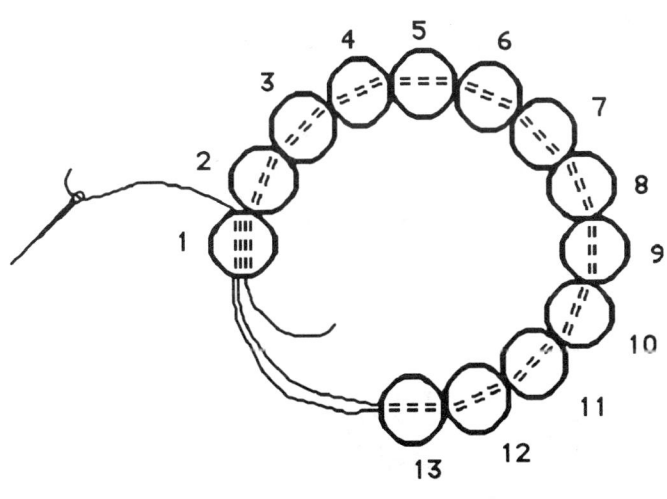

Row Two

5. Pick up a bead (#14) and pass the needle through bead #3.

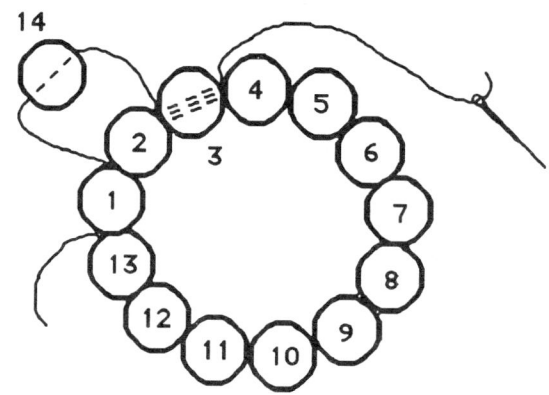

6. Pick up another bead (#15) and pass the needle through bead #5.

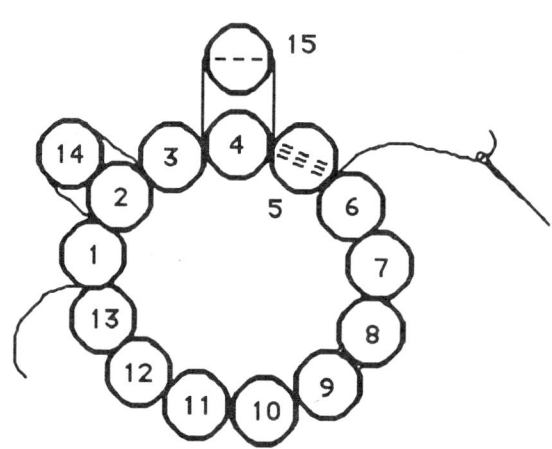

7. Pick up another bead (#16). Pass the needle through bead #7.

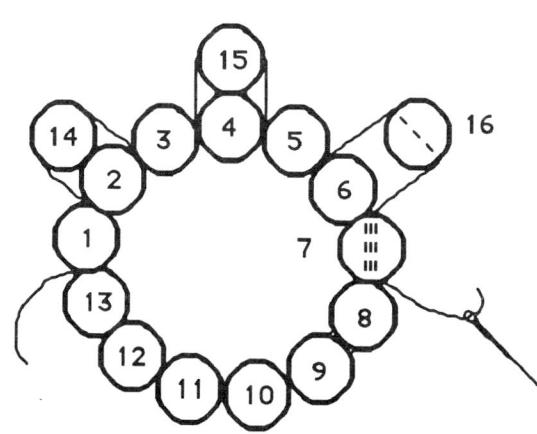

ROUND PEYOTE

(Odd-Numbered)

8. Continue in this manner for beads #17, #18 and #19 passing the needle through every other bead each time (#9, #11 and #13 respectively) as shown at right.

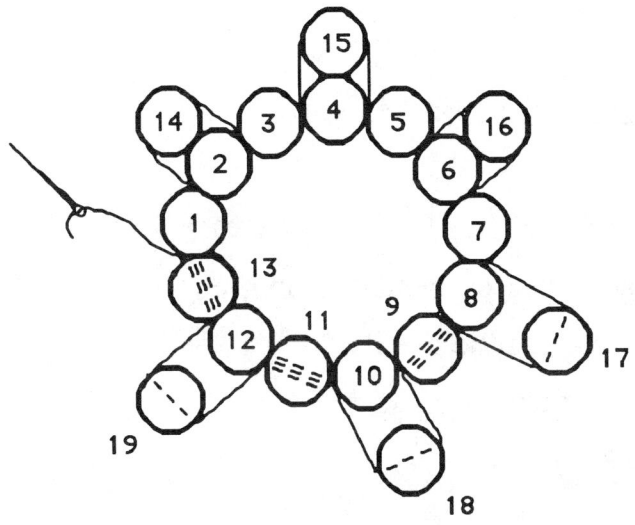

9. End this second row by picking up bead #20 and passing the needle through bead #14 (the first bead in Row Two). Pull the thread tight. There will be seven beads altogether in Row Two.

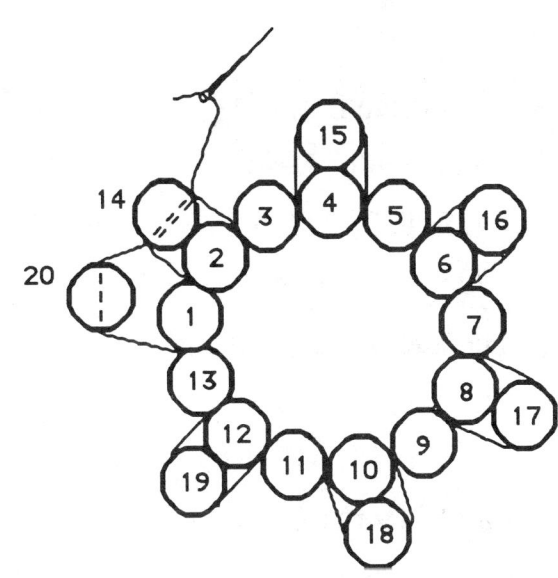

ROUND PEYOTE

(Odd-Numbered)

Row Three - Basket Row

10. Pick up bead #21 and pass the needle through bead #15.

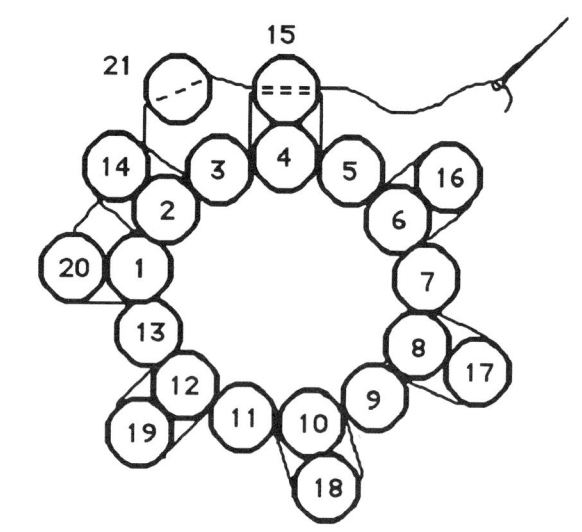

11. Continue in this manner for beads #22, #23, #24 and #25, passing the needle through a bead in Row Two each time (#16, #17, #18 and #19 respectively) as shown at right.

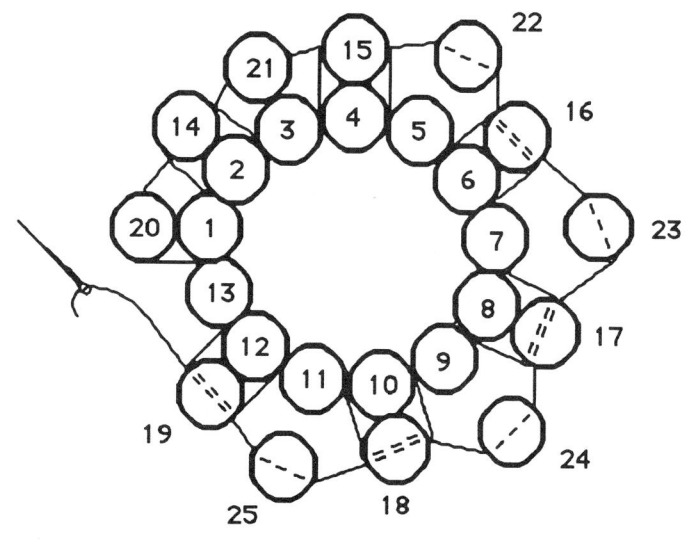

ROUND PEYOTE

(Odd-Numbered)

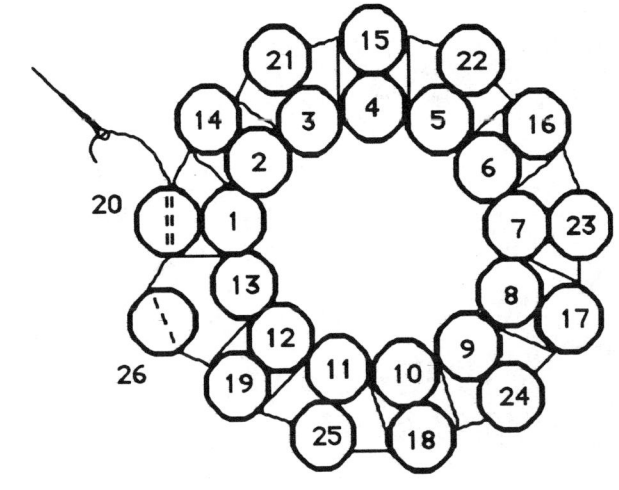

12. Pick up bead #26 and pass the needle through bead #20 to finish Row Three. Pull the thread tight.

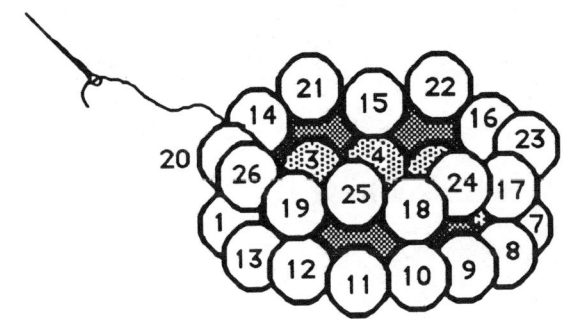

13. The work should now form a tube or basket as shown at right.

Row Four

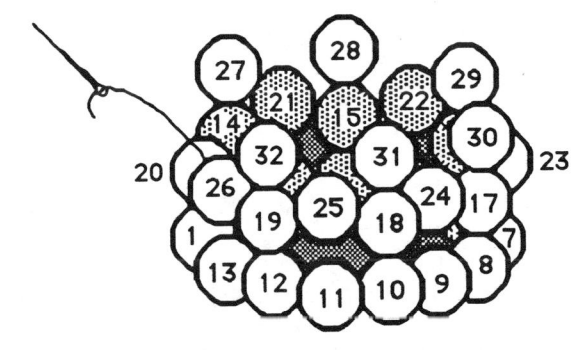

14. If it doesn't, add another row by repeating Steps 10 through 12 and adding six to all bead numbers.

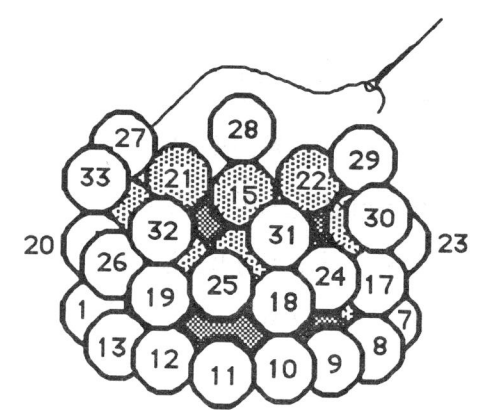

15. Pick up bead #33 and pass the needle through bead #27 to finish Row Four. Pull the thread tight.

Row Five - Basket Row

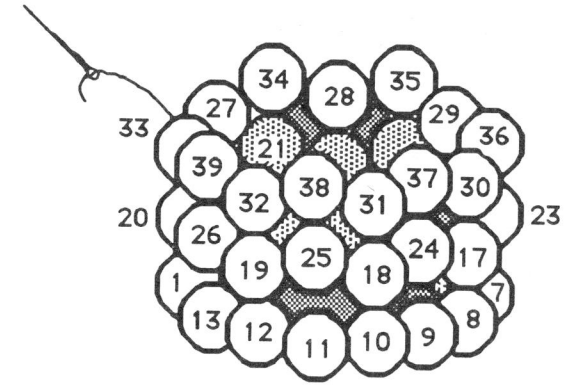

16. Repeat Steps 10 through 12 again but this time add thirteen to all bead numbers.

You may continue to add more rows by repeating Steps 10 through 12. Alternate between seven (even rows) and six (odd or basket rows) beads per row.

ROUND PEYOTE

(Odd-Numbered)

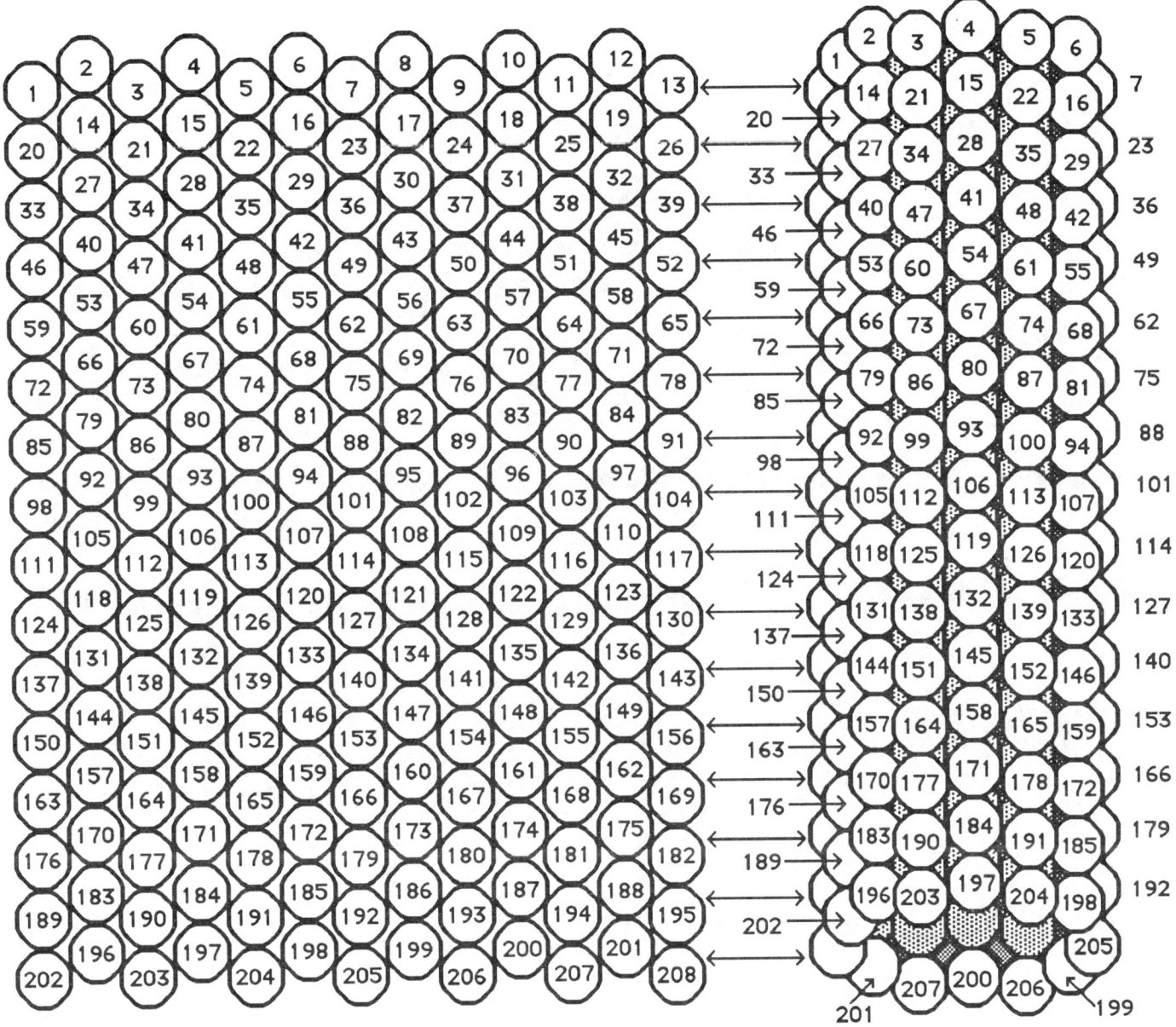

Copy this page and use colored pencils to create your own designs.

On the left side, the pattern has been 'cut' down one side and opened out flat. Use this section to work out your designs. The cylinder shown at the right has corresponding bead numbers so you can see how your design will look when it is finished.

CHAPTER 8

COMMANCHE STITCH

The Commanche is a very beautiful and majestic stitch. It is very versatile and one of my favorites. You can make a diamond-shaped earring if you use either all seed beads or all bugle beads. Another option is the triangle shape which usually works best when seed beads and bugle beads are both used and a fringe is added at the bottom row. Fringes can be very elaborate and you can incorporate some really nice designs with your fringe. Detailed fringe techniques are covered in Chapter Two (pg. 11).

COMMANCHE STITCH
(Brick - Laying)

1. Thread the needle with about two feet (two-thirds of a meter) of thread. Pick up a bugle bead on the needle. Pull the bead down the thread, leaving six to eight inches of thread as a tail. Now pass the needle through the bead again going in the same direction. Try not to split the thread as it will be removed later. See Starting and Finishing in Chapter One (pg. 4) for detailed explanations of this process.

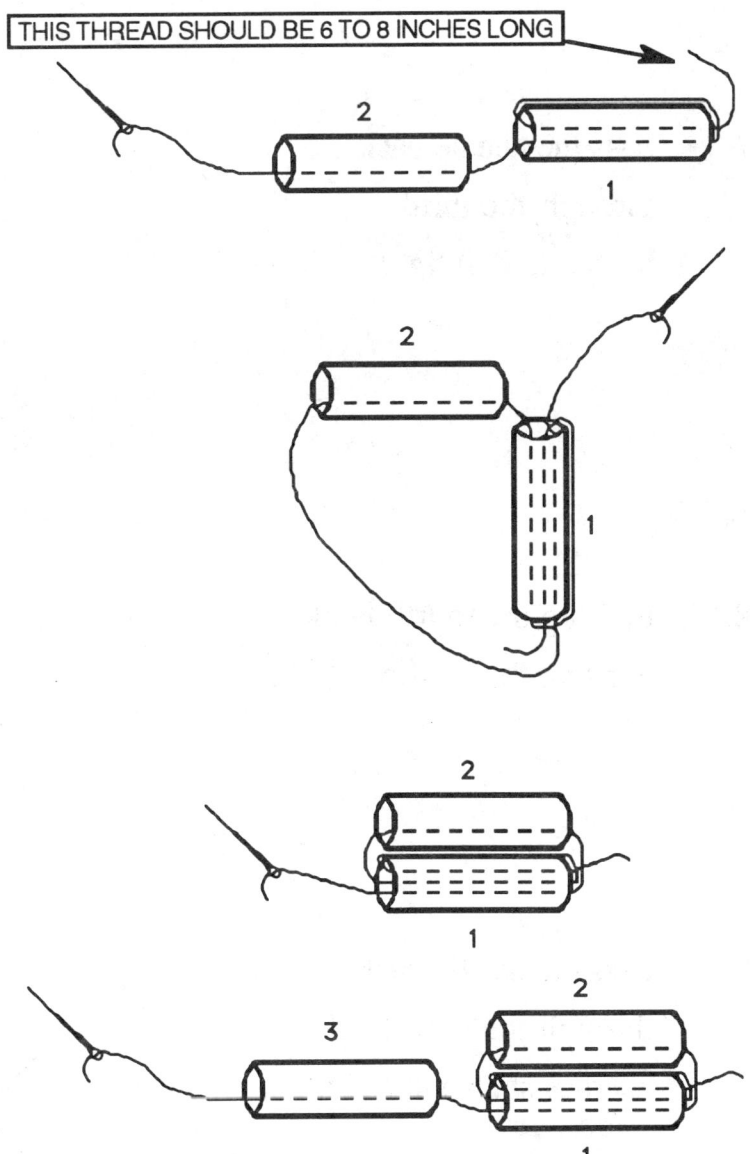

2. Pick up a second bugle bead on the needle. Let it drop down to the first bead.

3. Pass the needle back up through the first bugle bead as shown at right.

4. The two bugle beads now lay side by side.

5. Pick up the third bugle bead on the needle.

COMMANCHE STITCH
(Brick - Laying)

6. Pass the needle back through the first bead as shown at right. The thread is now emerging from the middle bead.

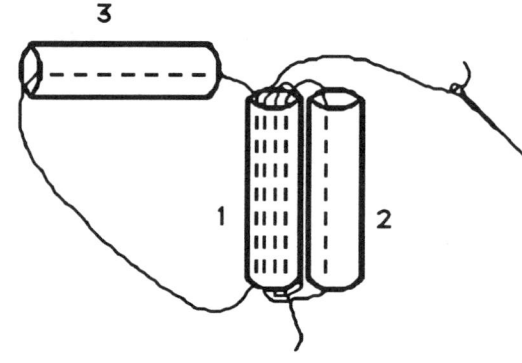

7. Pass the needle back through the third bead and pull tight.

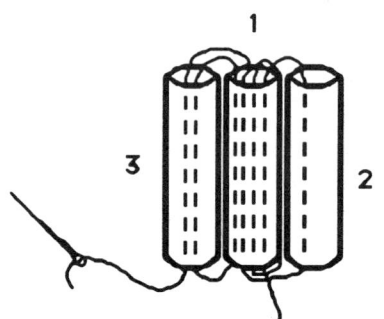

8. Pick up the fourth bugle bead on the needle.

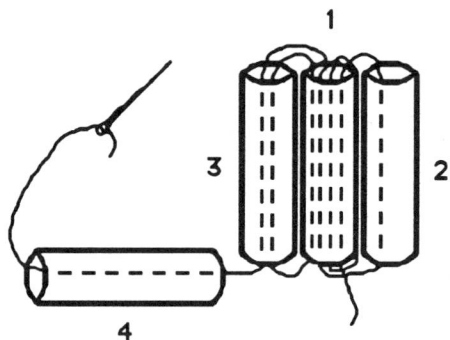

9. Pass the needle back through the third bugle bead as shown at right.

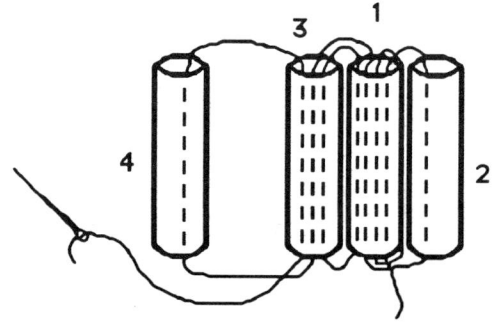

COMMANCHE STITCH
(Brick - Laying)

10. Pass the needle back through the fourth bead and pull tight.

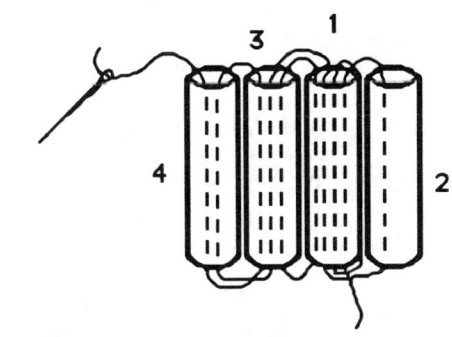

11. Pick up the fifth bugle bead on the needle.

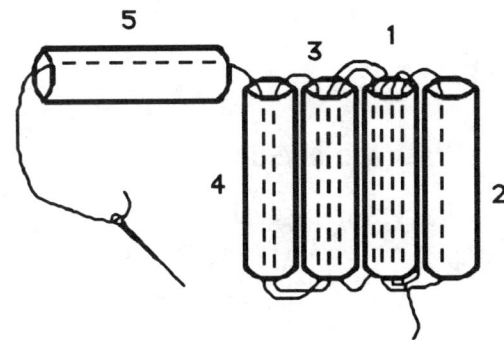

12. Pass the needle back through the fourth bugle bead.

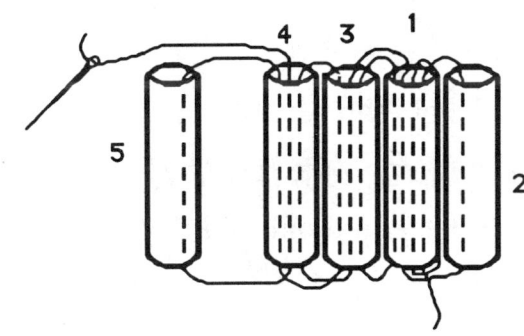

13. Pass the needle back through the fifth bugle bead and pull tight.

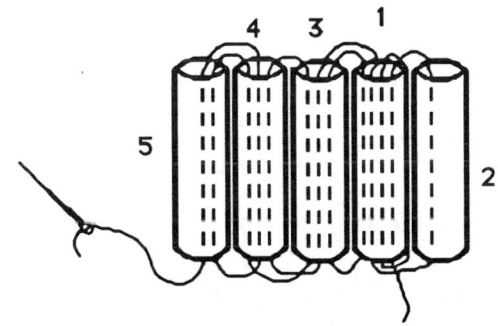

COMMANCHE STITCH
(Brick - Laying)

14. Pick up the sixth bugle bead on the needle.

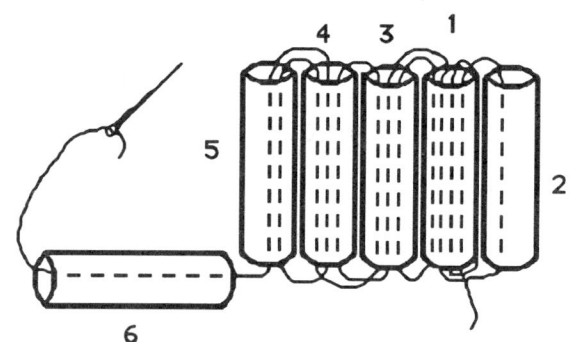

15. Pass the needle back through the fifth bugle bead.

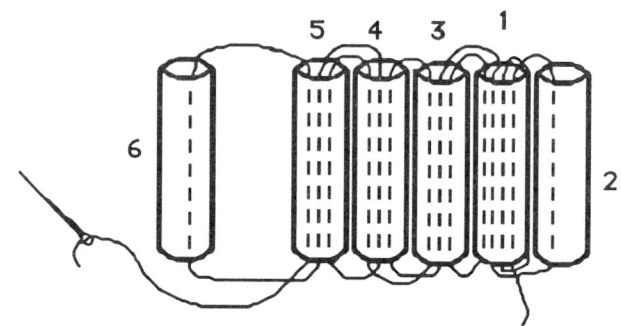

16. Pass the needle back through the sixth bugle bead and pull tight.

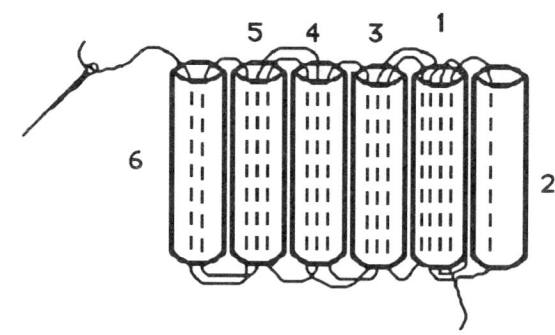

17. Pick up the seventh bead on the needle.

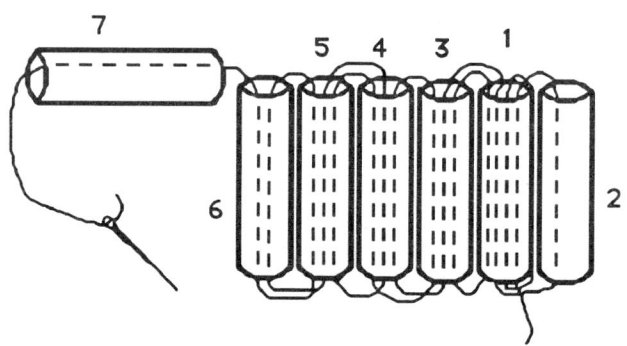

COMMANCHE STITCH
(Brick - Laying)

18. Pass the needle back through the sixth bugle bead.

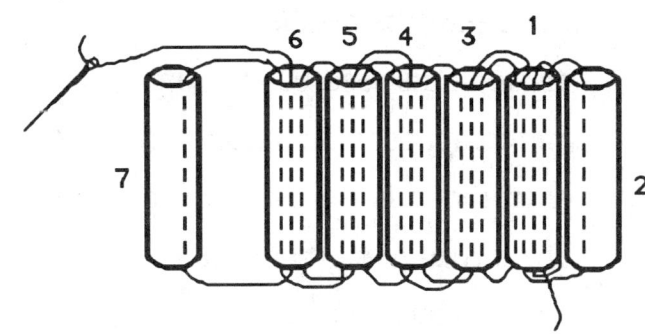

19. Pass the needle back through the seventh bead and pull tight.

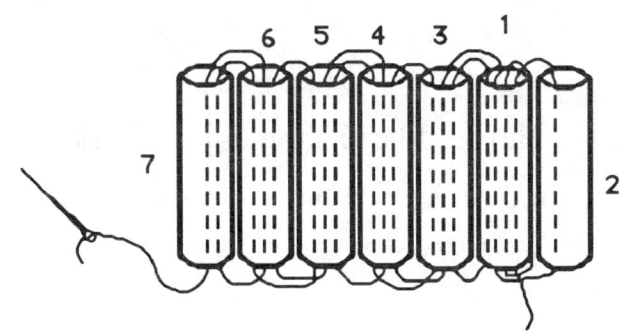

20. You are now ready to start the next section. Pick up a small seed bead (#8) on the needle.

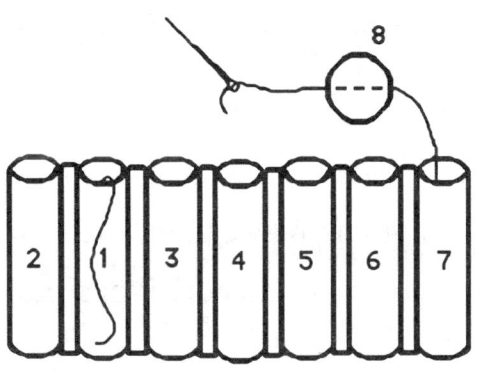

21. Pass the needle under the thread going between the last two bugle beads (#6 and #7). Pull tight. The seed bead now lies on top of the two bugle beads.

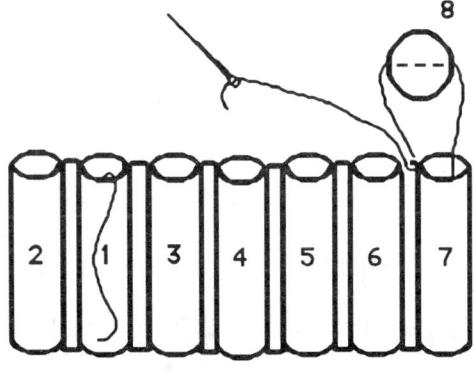

COMMANCHE STITCH
(Brick - Laying)

22. Now pass the needle back through the seed bead going in the opposite direction so that a loop is formed around the thread going between the two bugle beads.

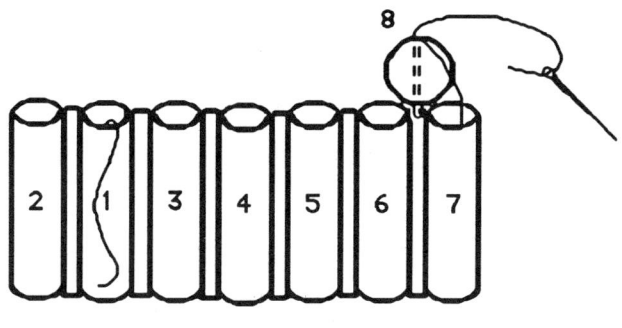

23. The seed bead should now lie flat on top of the two bugle beads. Pick up another small seed bead.

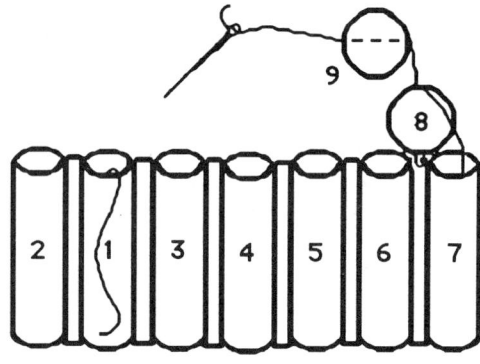

24. Pass the needle under the thread going between the next two bugle beads (#5 and #6) and pull tight.

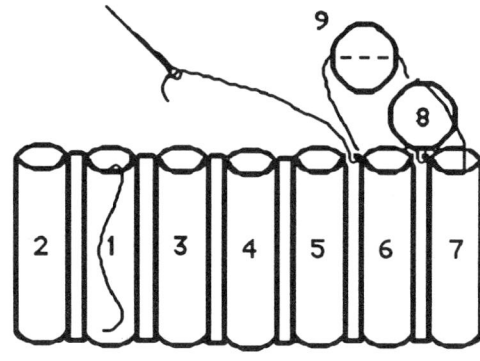

25. Pass the needle back through the second seed bead (#9) going in the opposite direction forming a loop around the thread as in step 22.

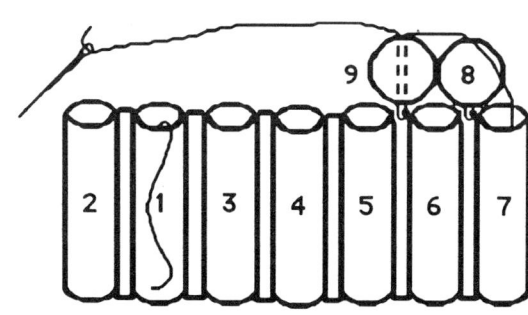

COMMANCHE STITCH
(Brick - Laying)

26. Repeat steps 23 through 25 four more times for a total of six seed beads in the first row of seed beads.

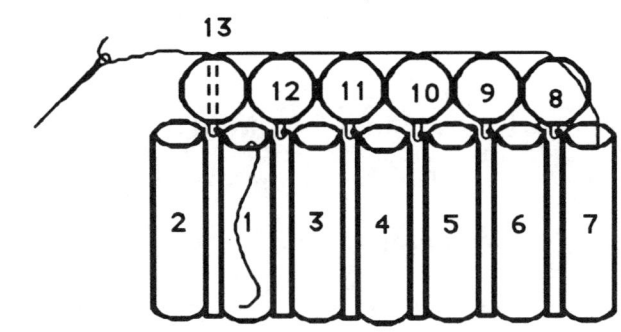

27. Pick up another seed bead to begin the next row of seed beads.

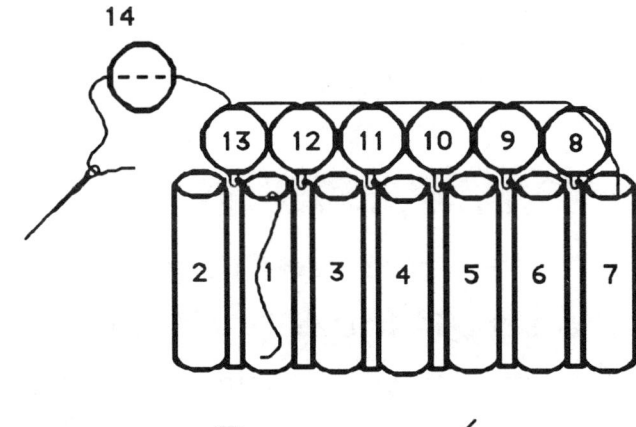

28. Pass the needle under the thread going between the last two seed beads (#12 and #13) in the first row of seed beads and pull tight.

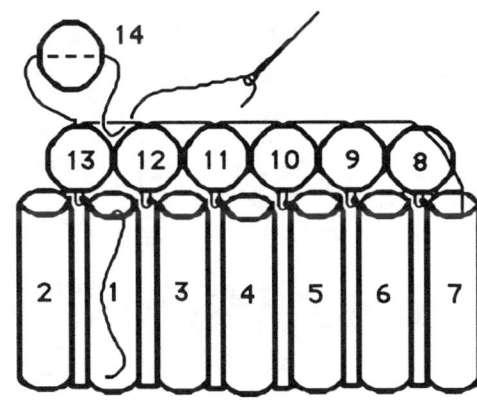

29. Pass the needle back through seed bead #14 going in the opposite direction and forming a loop around the thread going between seed beads #12 and #13.

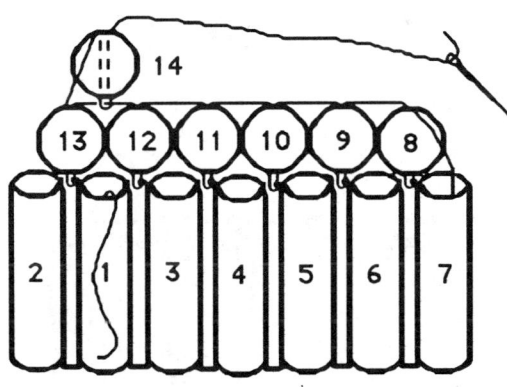

COMMANCHE STITCH
(Brick - Laying)

30. Repeat steps 27 through 29 four more times to complete the second row of seed beads. The thread now emerges from bead #18 in an upward direction.

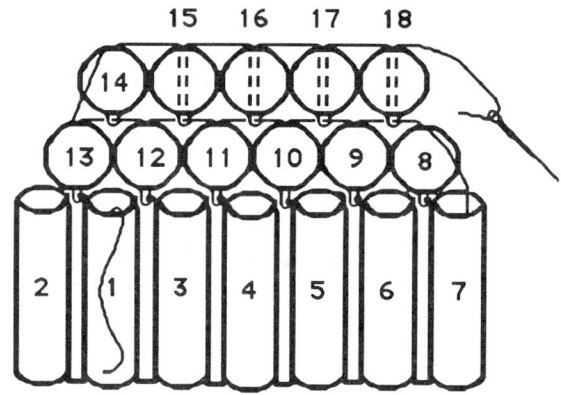

31. You are now ready to begin the third row of seed beads. Keep repeating steps 27 through 29, adding rows with one less bead each time until there are only two beads in the row.

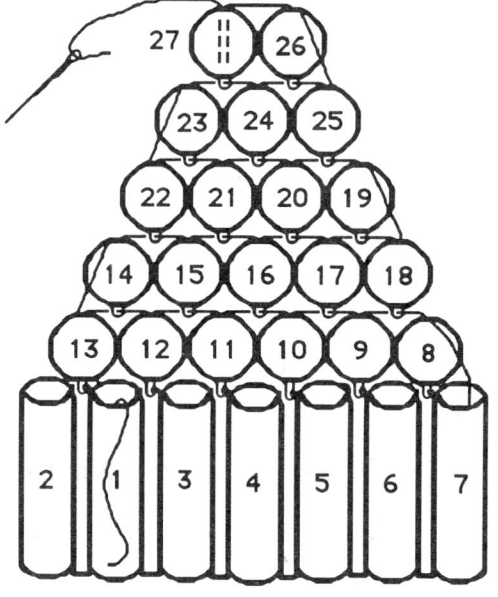

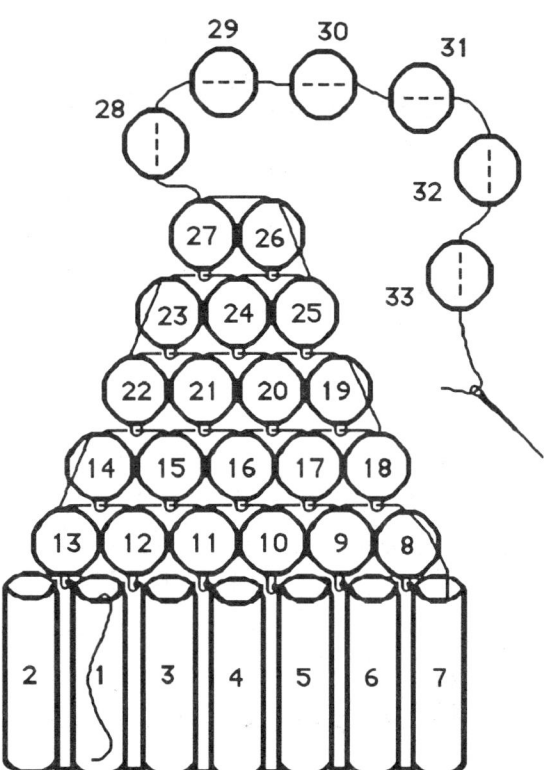

32. When the fifth row of seed beads consisting of two beads (#26 and #27) is completed, pick up six to eight seed beads on the needle (#28 through #33, #34 or #35, depending on how many beads you decide to use).

64

COMMANCHE STITCH
(Brick - Laying)

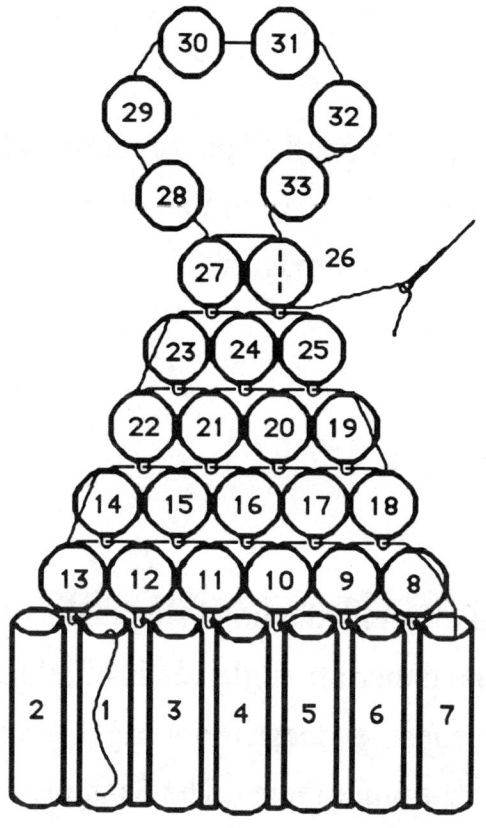

33. Now pass the needle downward through bead #26 and pull the thread tight.

34. Continue in this manner passing the needle through beads #25, #19, #18, #8 and #7 as shown below. Pull the thread tight after every bead. You have now completed the basic Commanche stitch, but there is finish work yet to do.

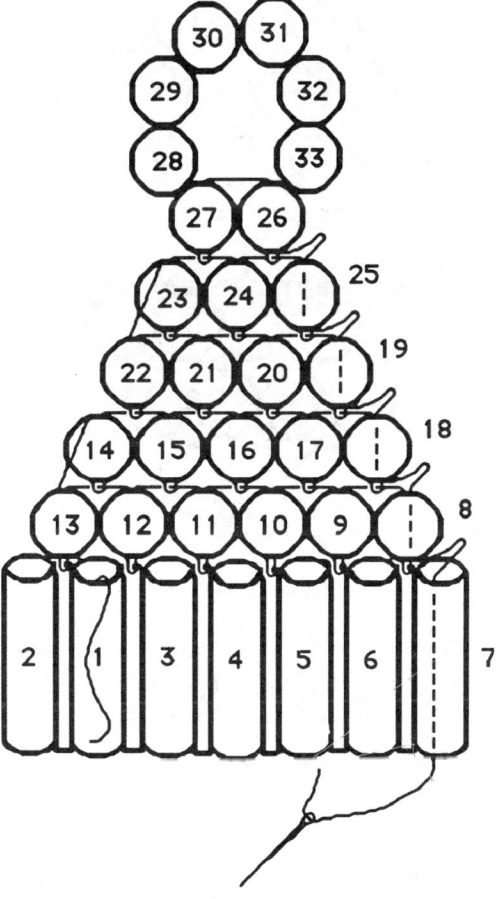

At this point you may want to work the thread emerging from bead #1 back into the piece using the zig-zag method described in the Starting and Finishing section of the first chapter in the book (pg. 4).

It is usual for the Commanche stitch to add some fringe to the bottom row. Many different fringe possibilities are explained in the second chapter of this book and are not covered in this chapter.

COMMANCHE STITCH
(Brick - Laying)

There is another option besides fringe. If you do not wish to add fringe to your piece, you may form a diamond shape by following the steps outlined below and on the next page.

To form a diamond shape, the beads must be either all bugle beads or all seed beads. It doesn't look right if you try to mix them. The example shown at the right uses all seed beads. Turn the work upside-down so that bead #7 is at the right side with the thread going upward from the top. Now go back and repeat steps 20 through 31. When you are finished, the work should look like the example shown at the right. The beads with no numbers represent that portion of the stitch which has already been completed. The numbered beads correspond with the bead numbers in steps 20 through 31. You are almost done.

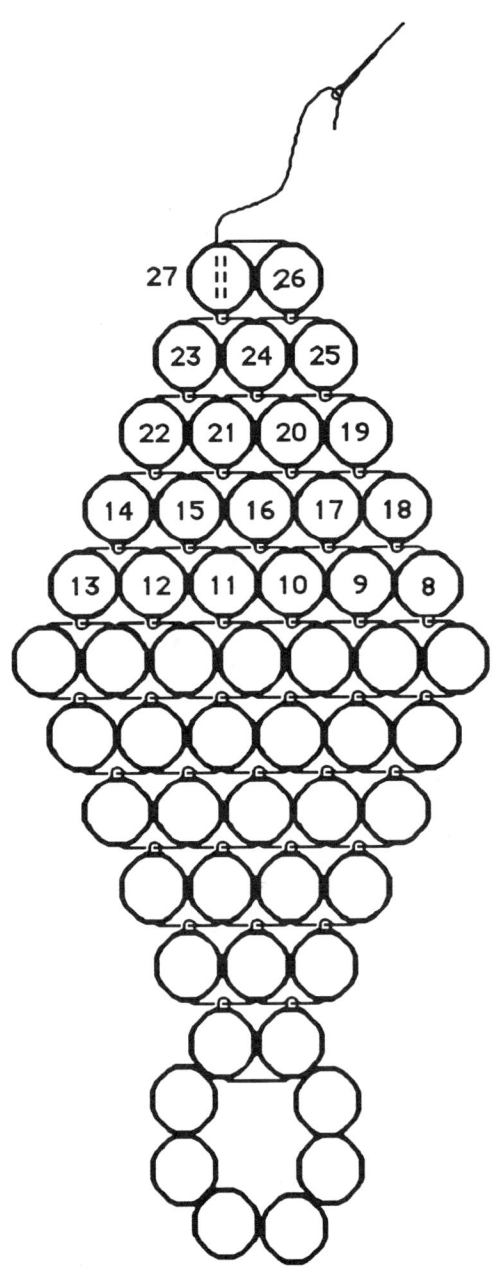

COMMANCHE STITCH
(Brick - Laying)

Now pick up one more seed bead (#28) and
pass the needle downward through seed
bead #26 as shown at right. Pull tight.

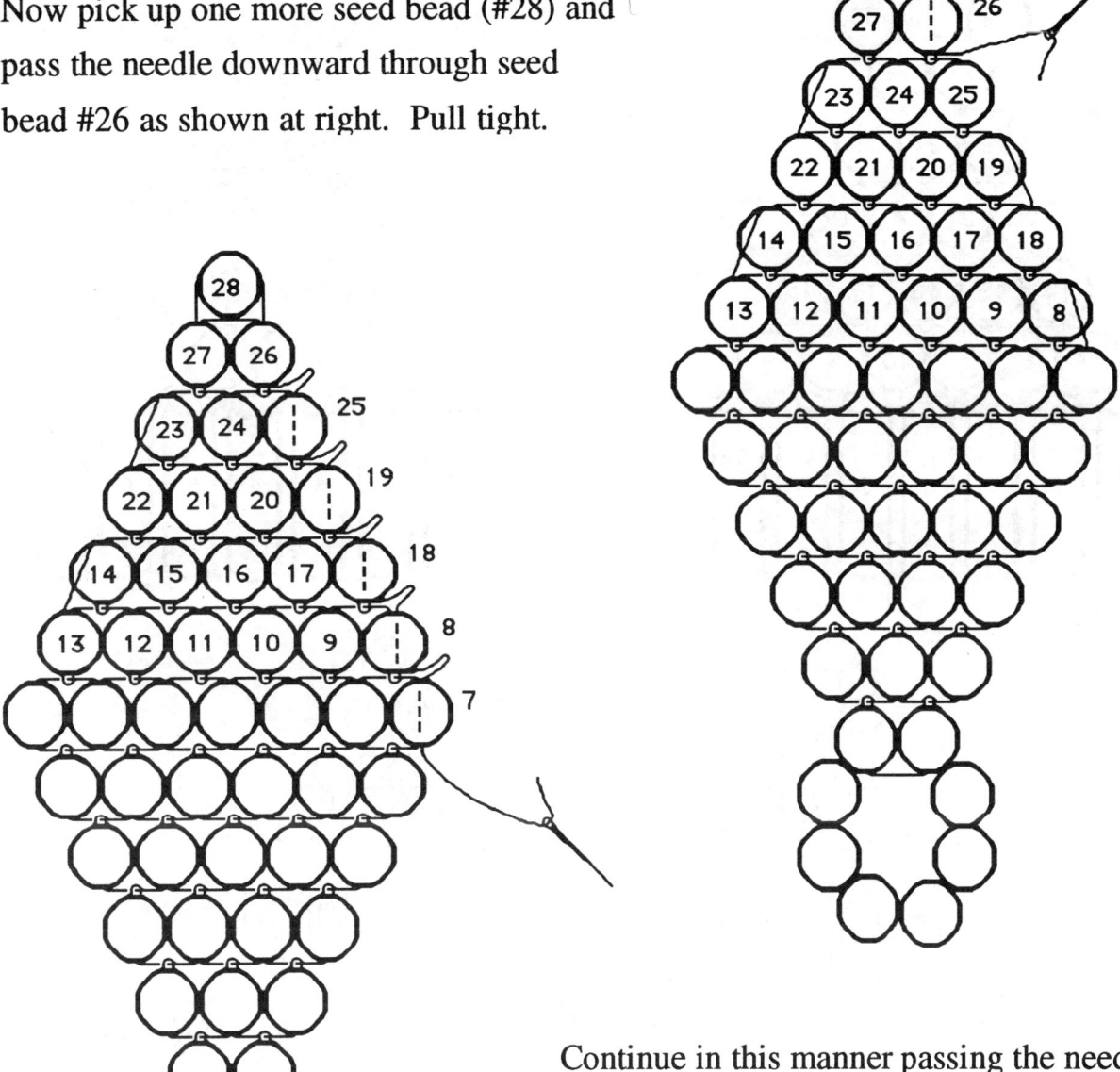

Continue in this manner passing the needle
downward through beads #25, #19, #18, #8 and
#7 as shown at left. Pull the thread tight after
every bead. When you have finished this last step,
work the remaining thread back into the piece
using the zig-zag method described in the Starting
and Finishing section of Chapter One (pg. 4).

COMMANCHE STITCH
(Brick - Laying)

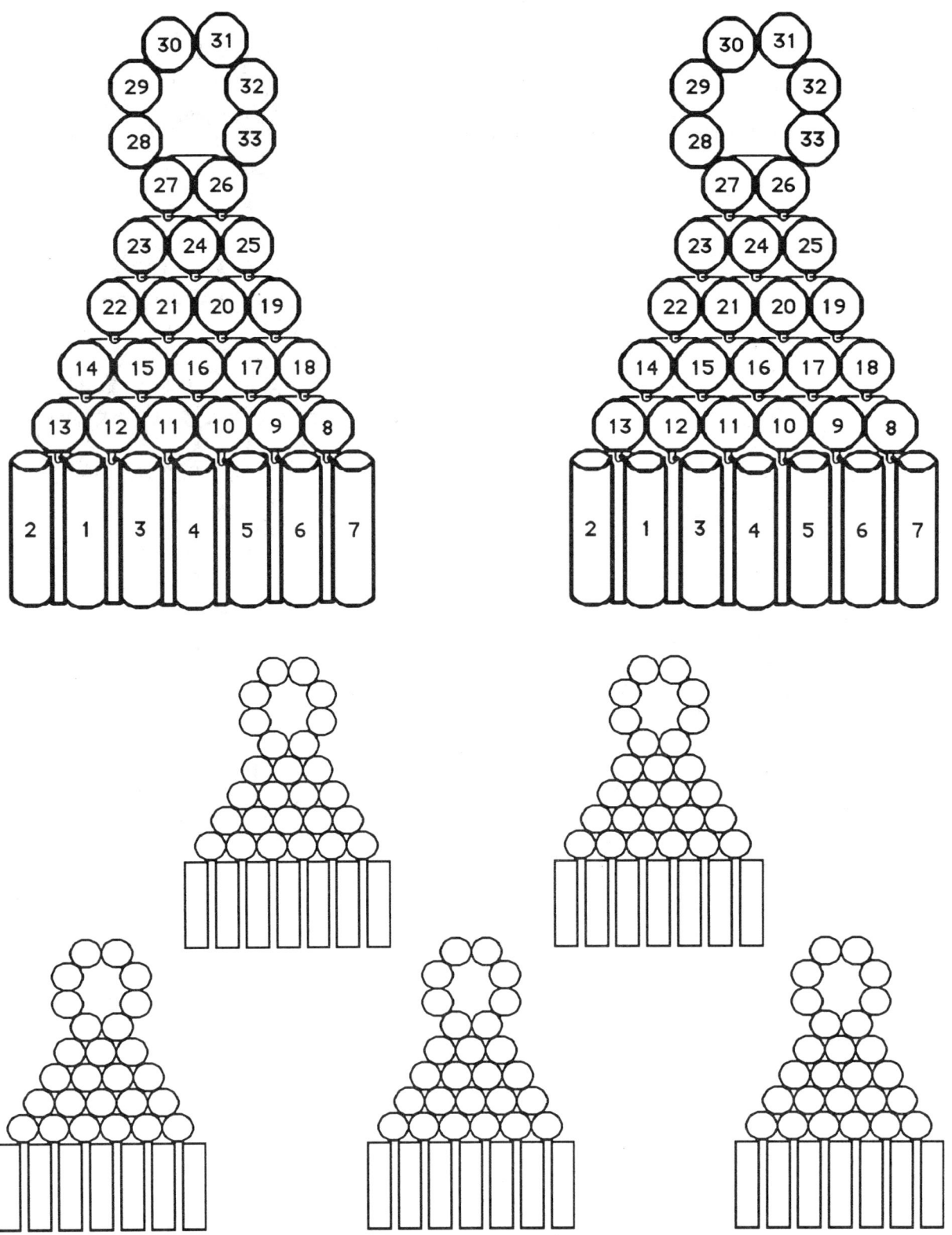

Copy this page and use colored pencils to create your own designs.

68

COMMANCHE STITCH

(Brick - Laying)

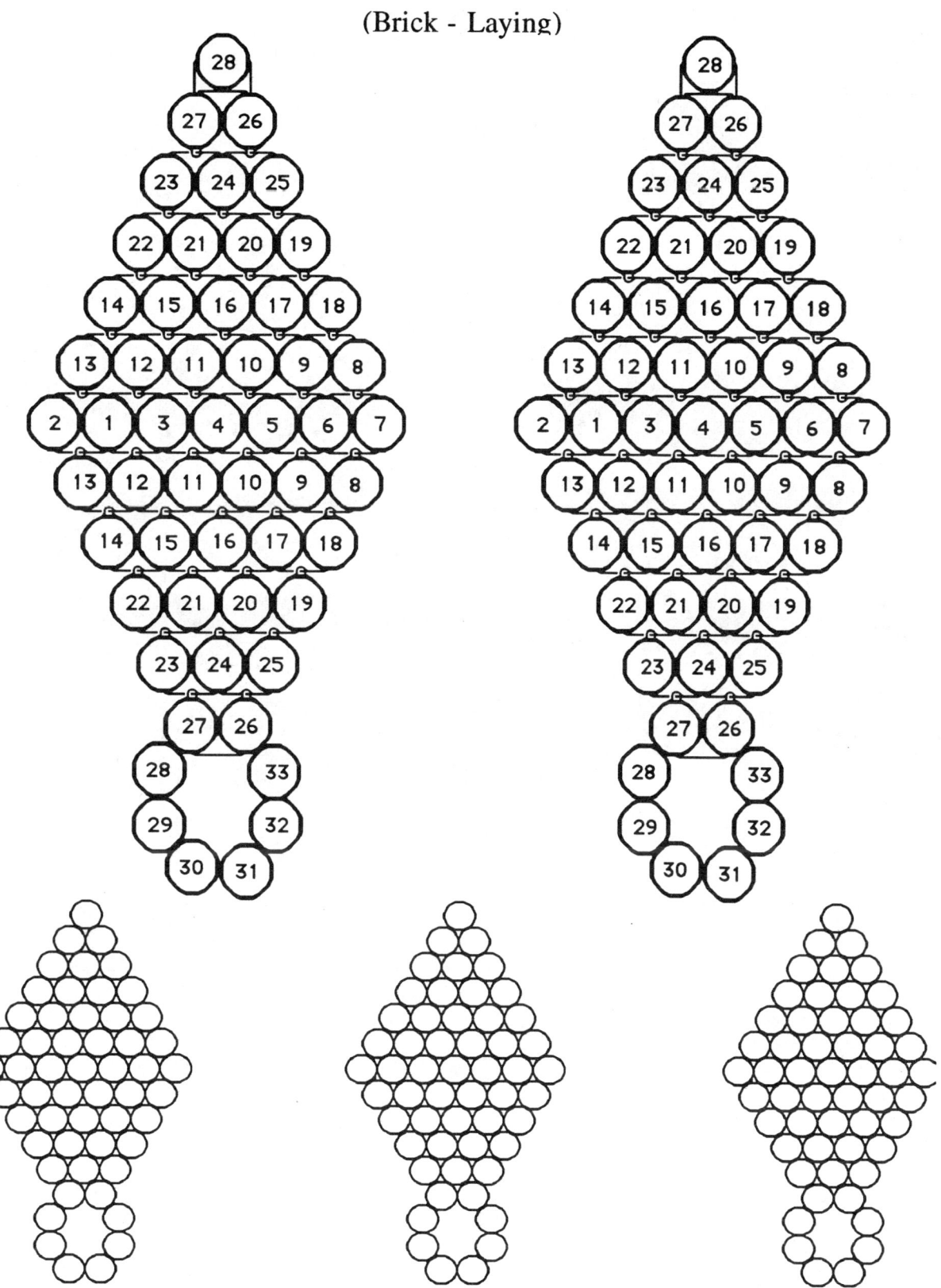

Copy this page and use colored pencils to create your own designs.

69

CHAPTER 9

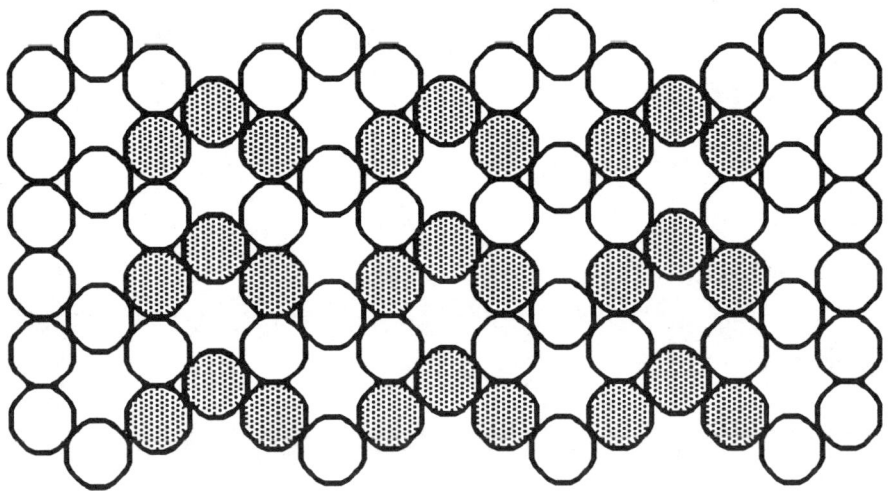

MEXICAN
LACE

The Mexican Lace stitch can be used for bracelets, anklets, earrings, chokers and bag covers. The thread tension for this particular stitch is critical. It must be moderately tight. You will probably have to try the stitch a few times before it comes out right so don't get too discouraged. Some very nice patterns can be incorporated into this lacy type of stitch. Use the pattern pages at the end of this chapter to experiment with different design ideas.

MEXICAN LACE

1.   Pick up a white bead on the needle. Pull the bead down the thread, leaving six to eight inches of thread as a tail. Now pass the needle up through the bottom of the bead. Try not to split the thread as it will be removed later. See Starting and Finishing in Chapter One (pg. 4) for detailed explanations of this process.

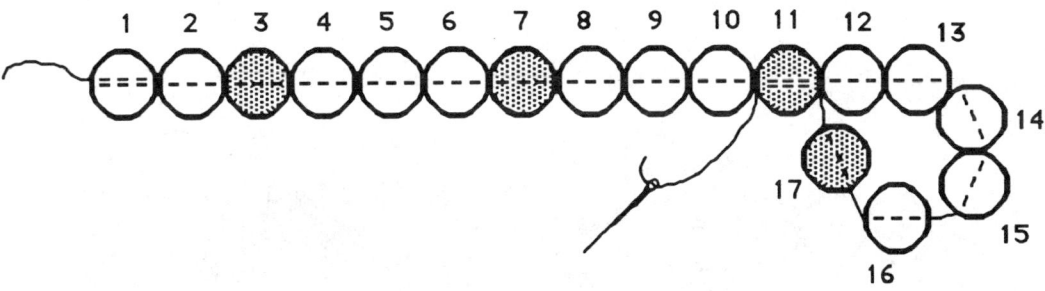

2.   Pick up sixteen more beads on the needle in the following order; 1 white, 1 black, 3 white, 1 black, 3 white, 1 black, 5 white and 1 black. Pass the needle back through bead #11 as shown above.

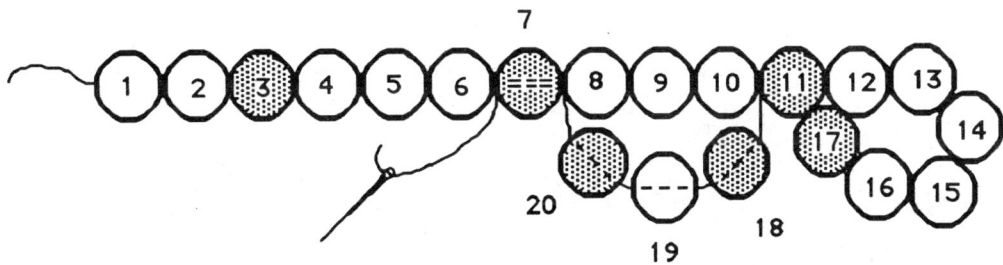

3.   Pick up 1 black, 1 white and 1 black bead (#18, #19 and #20) and pass the needle through bead #7 as shown above.

73

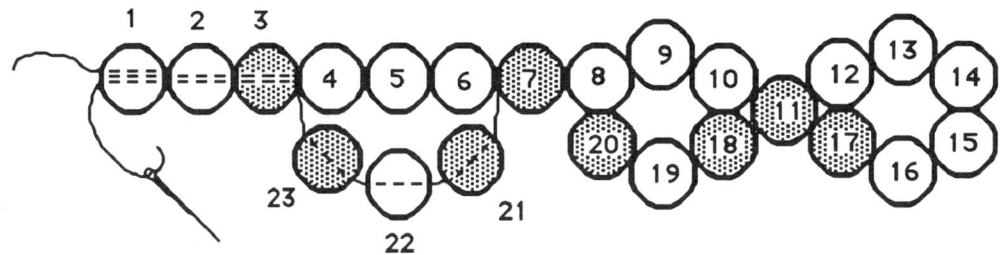

4. Pick up three more beads on the needle; 1 black (#21), 1 white (#22), and another black (#23). Pass the needle back through beads #3, #2 and #1.

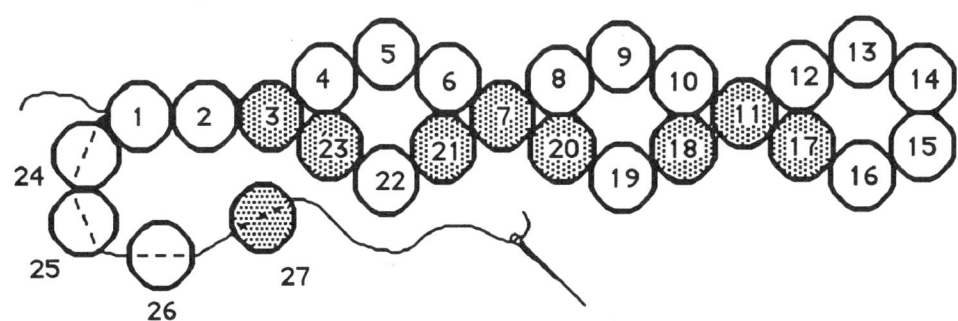

5. Pick up 3 white beads (#24, #25 and #26) and 1 black bead (#27).

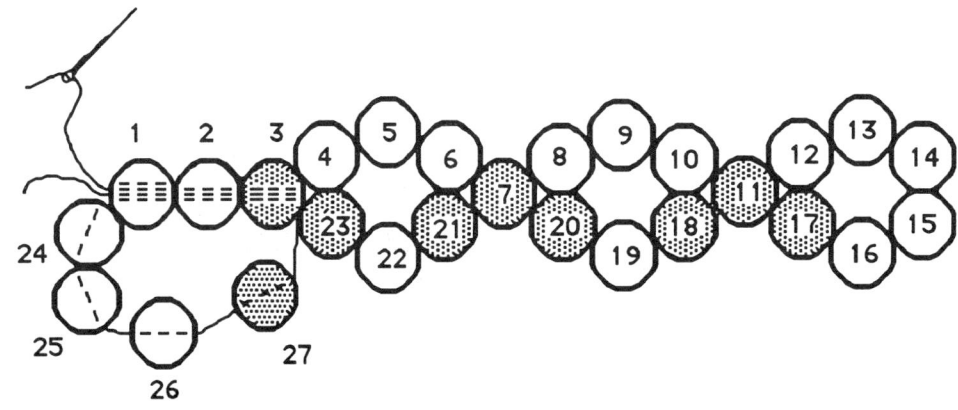

6. Pass the needle back through beads #3, #2 and #1 again.

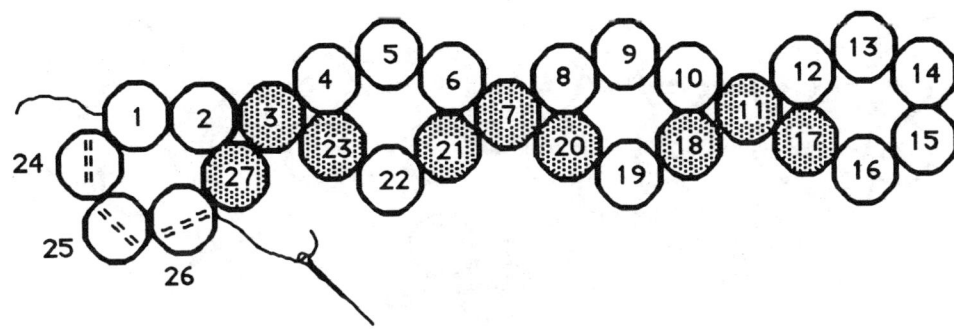

7.   Now pass the needle back through beads #24, #25 and #26.

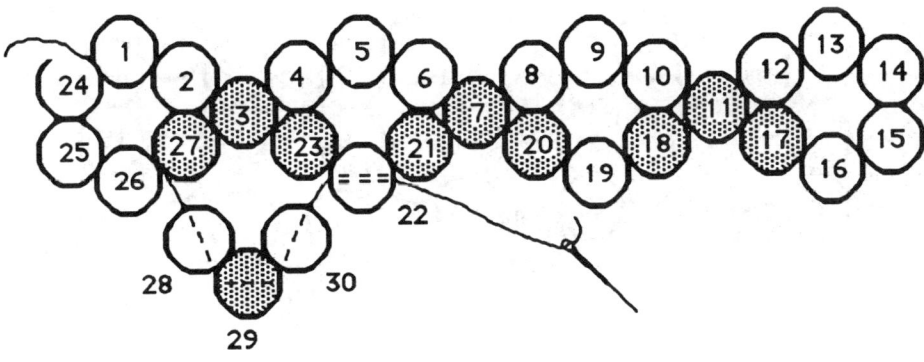

8.   Pick up 3 beads on the needle; 1 white (#28), 1 black (#29) and another white (#30). Pass the needle through bead #22.

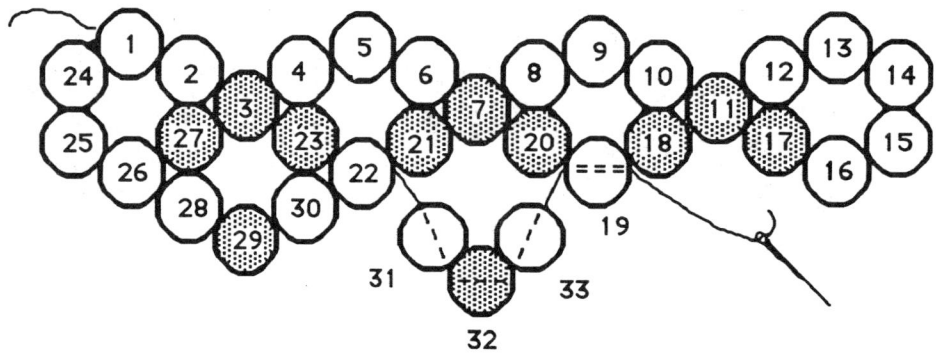

9. Pick up 3 more beads on the needle; 1 white (#31), 1 black (#32) and another white (#33). Pass the needle through bead #19.

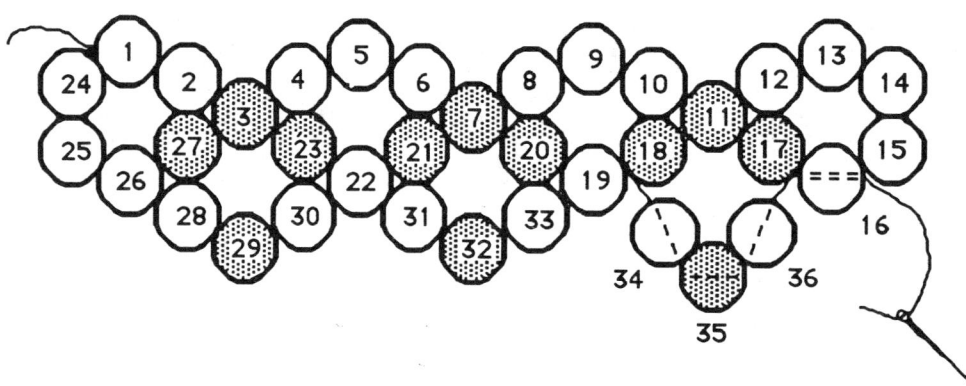

10. Pick up 3 more beads on the needle; 1 white (#34), 1 black (#35) and another white (#36). Pass the needle through bead #16.

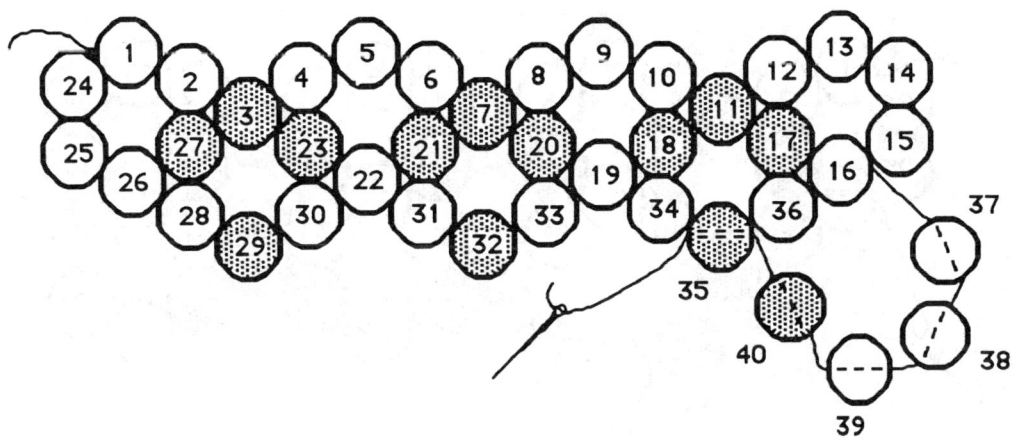

11.   Pick up 3 white beads (#37, #38 and #39) and 1 black bead (#40). Pass the needle back through bead #35 as shown above.

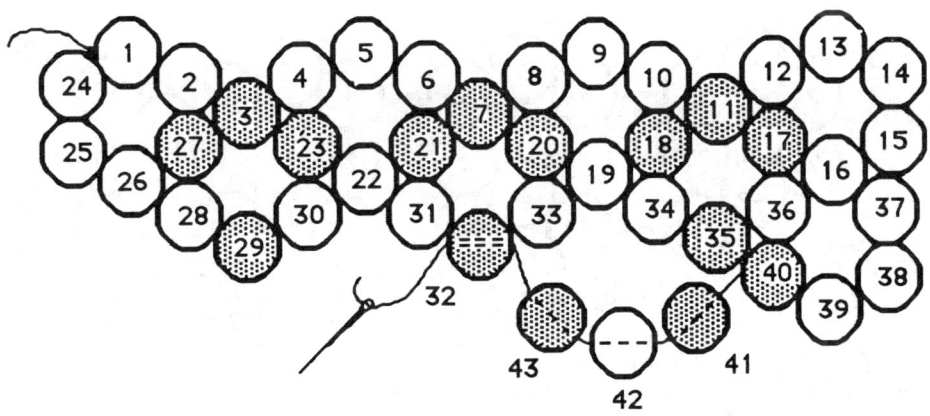

12.   Pick up 3 more beads on the needle; 1 white (#41), 1 black (#42) and another white (#43). Pass the needle through bead #32.

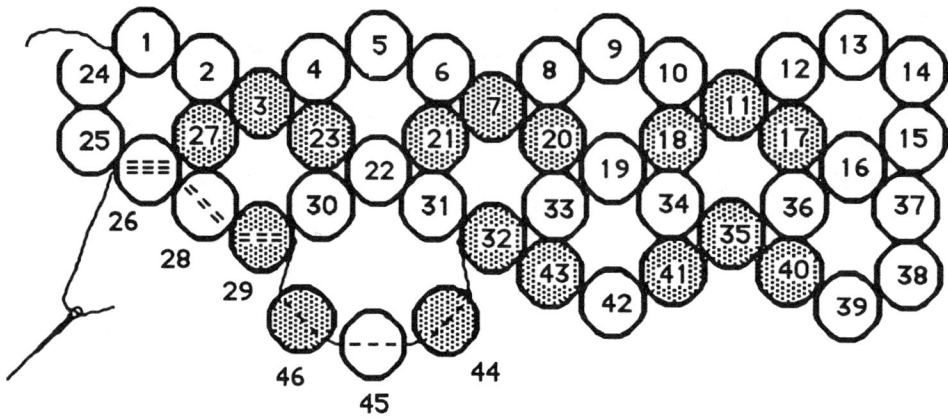

13.   Pick up 3 more beads on the needle; 1 black (#44), 1 white (#45) and 1 black (#46). Pass the needle through beads #29, #28 and #26.

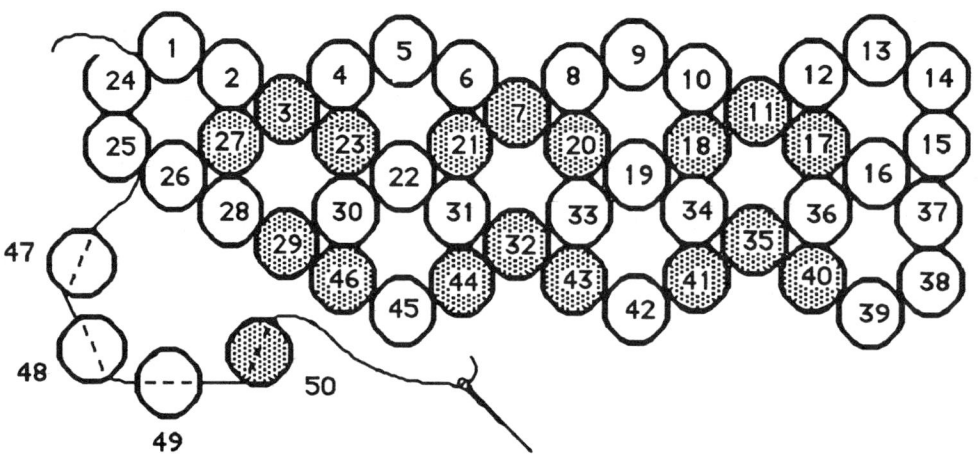

14.   Pick up 3 white beads (#47, #48 and #49) and 1 black bead (#50).

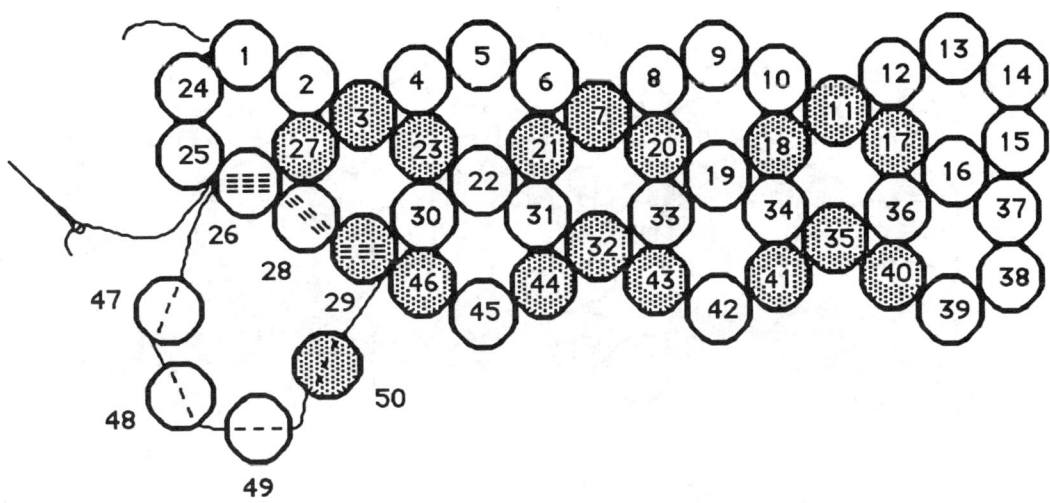

15. Pass the needle back through beads #29, #28 and #26.

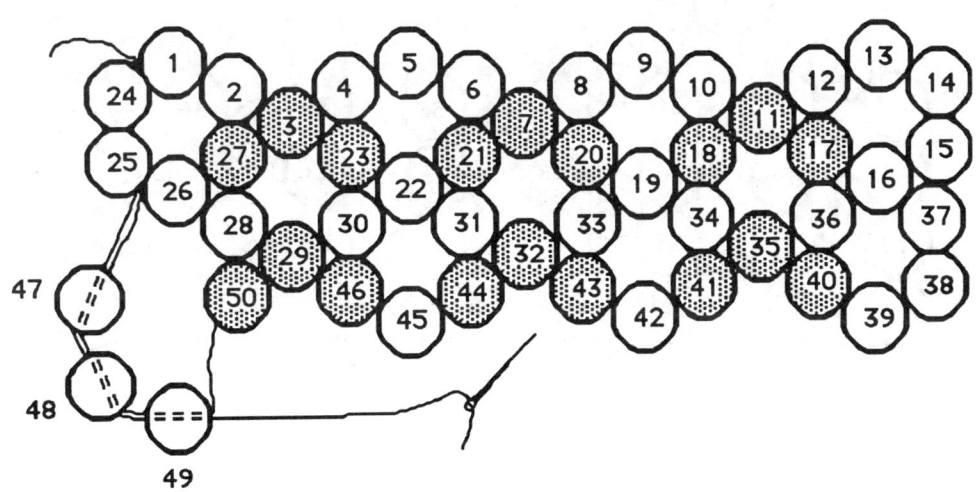

16. Now pass the needle through beads #47, #48 and #49.

MEXICAN LACE

The piece should now look like the example shown below.

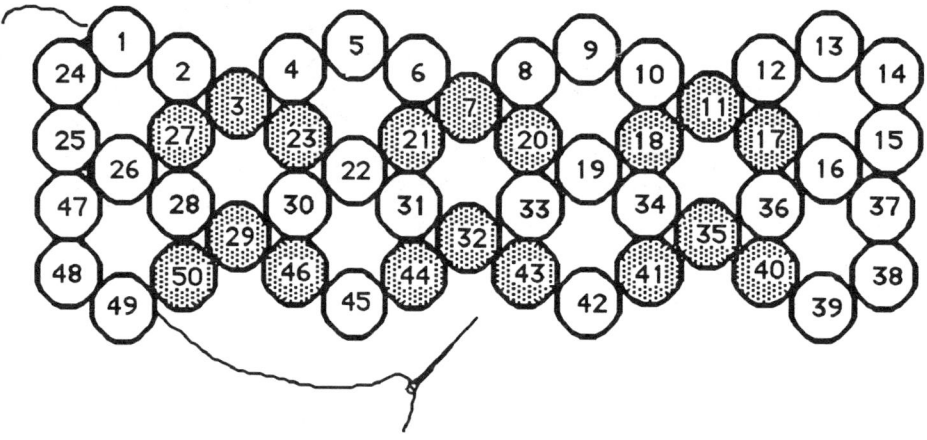

Repeat steps 8 through 16 to add another row.

Add 23 to all bead numbers.

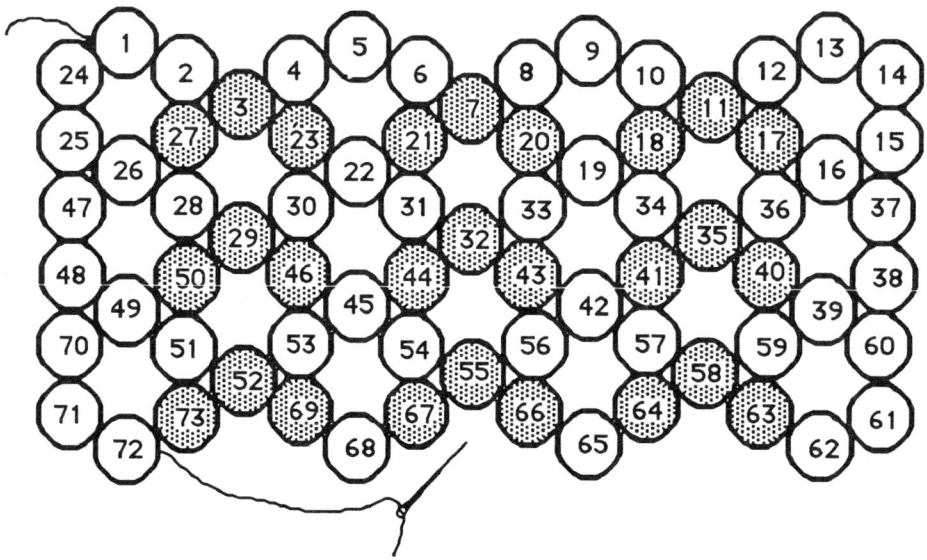

Keep repeating steps 8 through 16 to continue adding rows. Be sure to add 23 to all bead numbers each time.

MEXICAN LACE

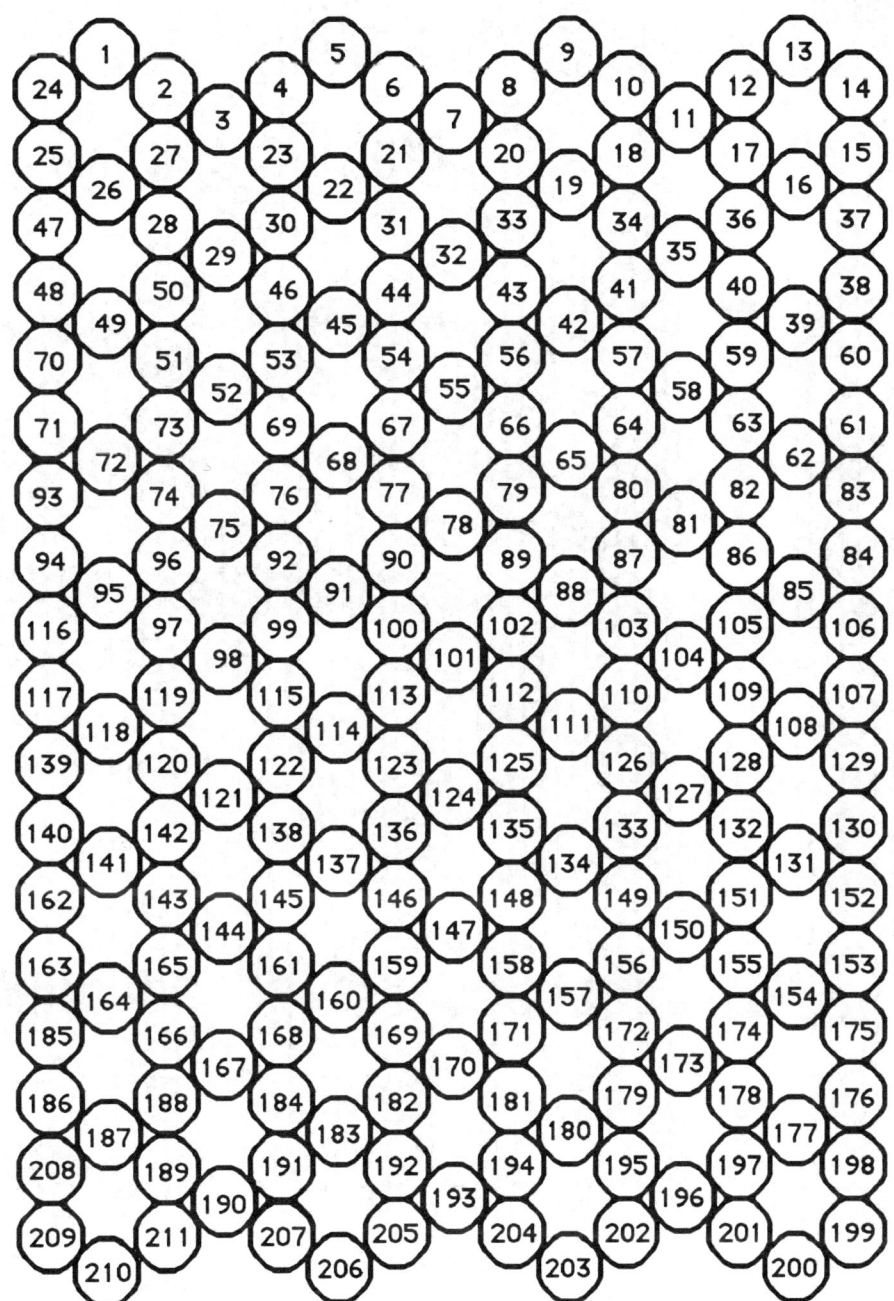

Copy this page and use colored pencils to create your own designs.

81

MEXICAN LACE

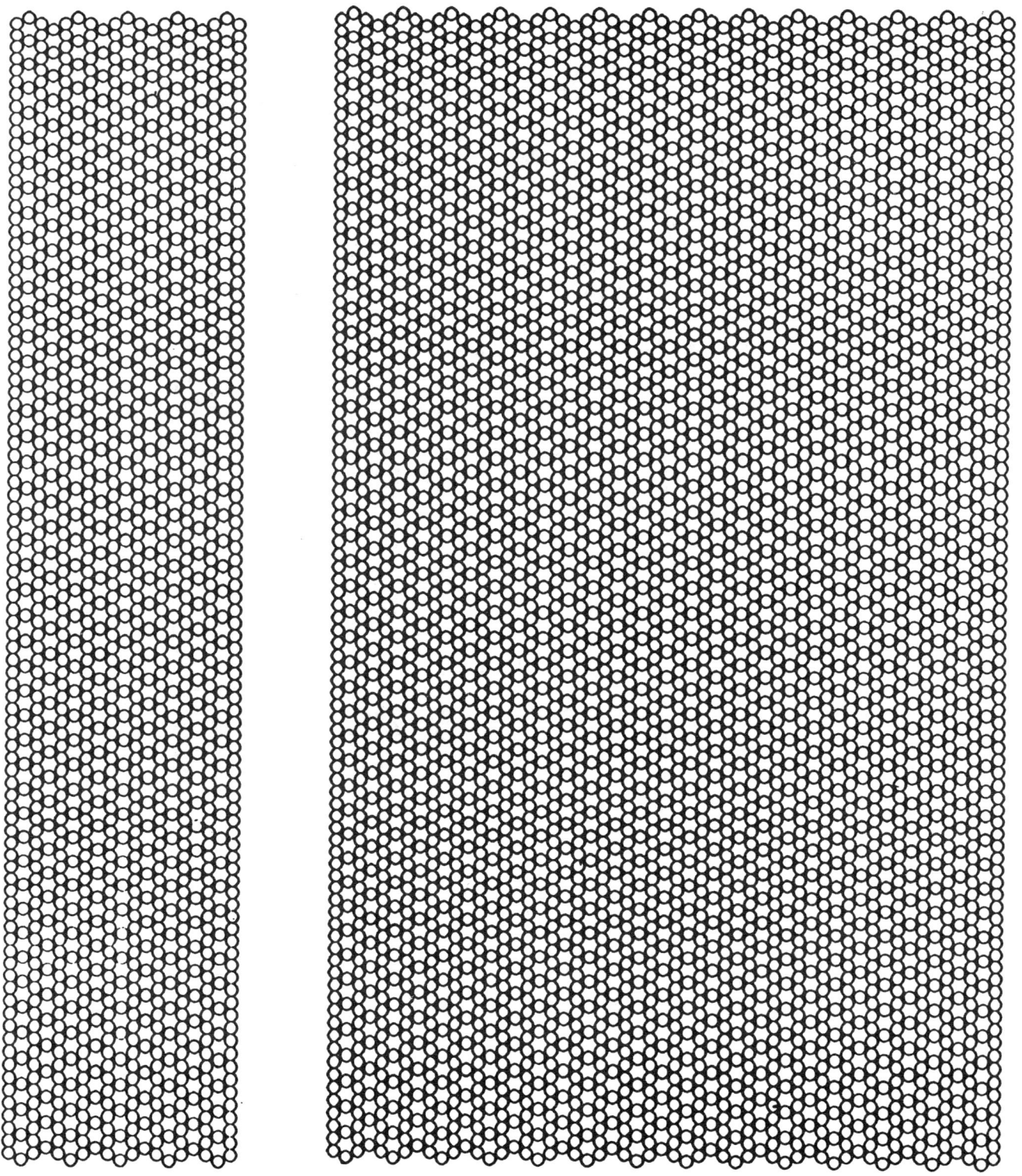

Copy this page and use colored pencils to create your own designs.

GLOSSARY

African Flower Mandala

see Flower Mandala

aught - (awt)

This is a term used to designate bead sizes. It is preceded by a number ranging from 8 to 25. The symbol for aught is the degree sign [°]. The larger the number, the smaller the bead size. The term 25° (twenty-five aught) would indicate the smallest size of bead available.

barrel clasp

This consists of two halves which screw together forming a barrel shape. Each half is usually attached to a bead tip.

BARREL CLASP

bead

This can be any object with a hole drilled through it. There are many different sizes and shapes of beads. See specific listings for more in-depth descriptions of the different kinds of beads.

bead tip

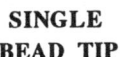
SINGLE BEAD TIP

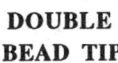
DOUBLE BEAD TIP

Using bead tips is accepted as the professional method of starting and finishing a bracelet, necklace or anklet. It gives added strength to the main piece and puts less stress on the clasp. After the bead tip has been attached, the clasp is then attached to the hook on the bead tip and the hook is bent shut.

brick-laying

This is a style of beading in which the rows of beads are staggered just like bricks. It is the main technique used in the Commanche stitch (pg. 55).

GLOSSARY

bugle bead

These are beads with a cylindrical or tube-like shape. They are one of the most common types of bead. They range in length from 3/8 of an inch to 2 inches. They are used primarily in brick-laying stitches and fringes. They come in many different colors and are made from various materials, the most common being glass and metal.

Chevron Chain

This stitch is used primarily in necklaces, bracelets and anklets. It can be done with seed beads and bugle beads or seed beads alone.

clasp

There are many kinds of clasps. They fall into the category of findings. They usually consist of two metal pieces which are attached to either end of the beadwork. They may then be attached to or detached from each other so the piece may be worn. Some of the types include barrel, hook and eye, jump-ring and spring-ring clasps. See individual listings for more detailed descriptions.

Commanche stitch

This is a stitch commonly used to make earrings and pendants. It employs brick-laying techniques and usually has fringe added. It can be done with seed beads, bugle beads or a mixture of both.

Daisy Chain

This stitch is used primarily in necklaces, bracelets and anklets. It is always done with seed beads.

double-stick tape

This is simply tape that is sticky on both sides. It is used to hold your piece to the table while doing other work on it such as adding fringe or findings.

Even-numbered Peyote

see Flat Peyote (pg. 85)

GLOSSARY

earring hook

Thesc are a type of finding and are available in two styles; earwire and shephard's hooks.

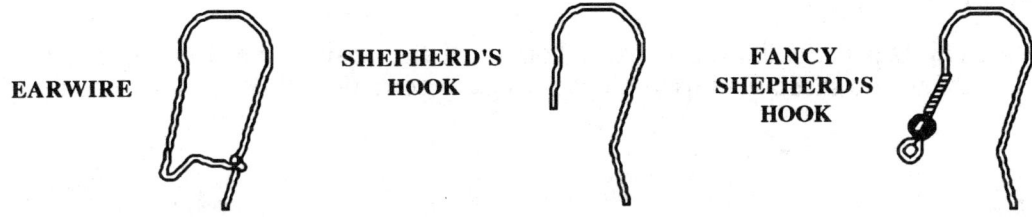

EARWIRE   SHEPHERD'S HOOK   FANCY SHEPHERD'S HOOK

earwire

see earring hook

eye clasp

see hook and eye clasp

findings

These are the metal pieces which are attached to the beadwork so that it can be fastened and worn. These include bead tips, barrel clasps, hook-and-eye clasps, spring-ring clasps, jump-ring clasps, and earring hooks. See individual listings for more detailed descriptions.

Flat Peyote stitch

This stitch is used for bracelets, anklets, belts and even pictures if you are highly ambitious. This is a brick-laying technique. Seed beads are used for this stitch.

Flower Mandala

This stitch is used in earrings and pendants. It is done with seed beads and may have fringe added to it.

fringe

This is a series of beaded strings which hang from the edge of a piece of beadwork intended to enhance the design. The fringe can be any length. The length can vary from string to string, giving a graduated effect, or remain consistent for straight fringe. It may be incorporated into many different stitch designs. More detailed explanations can be found in Chapter 2 (pg. 11).

GLOSSARY

glue

    see super-glue, jeweler's glue and Krazy-glue

graph paper

    This is paper with evenly spaced horizontal and verticle lines forming a grid pattern over the whole sheet. It is useful in working out complicated designs, especially fringe designs.

hank

    This is a term which describes a quantity of beads. There are usually 8 to 12 individual strands on a hank of beads.

hook and eye clasp

    This type of finding makes the piece easy to clasp and unclasp but also makes it easy to fall off your wrist or ankle. They are usually attached with bead tips.

HOOK

EYE

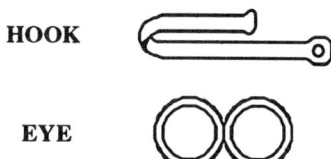

Indian Flower

    see Daisy Chain (pg. 84)

jewelers' glue

    see super-glue

jump-ring clasp

    This is simply a ring of metal. It is a type of finding that is used along with a spring-ring to form a clasp for necklaces, bracelets and anklets. It is usually attached with a bead tip.

JUMP-RING

Krazy-glue

    Avoid this type of glue as it is too runny.

Mandala

    see Flower Mandala (pg. 85)

GLOSSARY

Mexican Lace

This stitch can be used in earrings, as a cover for a bag or even a belt if you are ambitious. It is made with seed beads.

needle

Beading needles range in size from #10 (thickest) through #16 (thinnest). Different companies guage their needles differently so it is a good idea to take the beads you will be using along with you when you buy needles and actually pass one of the needles through a bead to make sure the needle is slender enough.

needle threader

This is a device which can be purchased at many craft stores which sell beads and needles. It is useful for the larger needle sizes but doesn't work well (if at all) for the smaller sizes.

Odd-numbered Peyote

see Round Peyote (pg. 87)

peyote

This is a term for a brick-laying technique. It can be flat or round (cylindrical) and it can be odd-numbered or even-numbered which is important in design considerations, especially for the round peyote stitch.

Round Peyote

This stitch can be used in earrings, bracelets, necklaces and covers for drawstring bags. It uses seed beads and the finished product is in the shape of a cylinder.

seed bead

This is the most common type of bead and there are numerous sizes and types of seed beads. It is generally spherical in shape. In the past, beads were made by drilling holes through various types of seeds. This is where the name comes from.

shepherd's hook

see earring hook

GLOSSARY

spring-ring clasp

This is a type of finding that is used along with a jump-ring to form a clasp for necklaces, bracelets and anklets. It is usually attached with a bead tip.

strand

This is a single string of beads. It is usually 8 to 12 inches long. The number of beads on a strand will vary according to the size of the beads. There are 8 to 12 strands on a full hank of beads which is usually the quantity by which they are sold.

Super-glue

This is a very strong glue which is useful in attaching findings more securely to the beadwork. Use it sparingly.

tape

see double-stick tape

thread

Thread is what holds a beadwork piece together. It comes in a variety of thicknesses from size triple A (which is the thinnest) to size G (the thickest). The appropriate thread size for a given piece will depend on the size of the beads being used and the number of times the thread must pass through a bead. Thread can be bought waxed or unwaxed.

threader

see needle threader

Twill Stitch

see Flat Peyote (pg. 85)

INDEX

INDEX

INDEX

INDEX

INDEX

Smithsonian likes beadwork

By Neita Cecil

Staff writer

MAUPIN — Thinking it was a magazine solicitation, Desiree Vinson almost threw out the envelope with the Smithsonian Institution logo.

But curiosity won out and she opened the letter, only to find herself holding an invitation to enter her intricate beadwork in the Smithsonian's national traveling beadwork exhibit.

She did — reluctantly, after prodding by friends — but never got around to seeing the show. In fact, Vinson, never a stickler for dates, is not quite sure what year it was: 1988 or 1989.

By then, the Jamaican native, now a Maupin resident, had done beadwork for a decade and earned a living from it for half that time.

Told as a child her dreams of being an artist were foolish, and that she had no talent anyway, Vinson spent years perfecting her beadwork before it dawned on her that her dream had come true.

But it was never her goal to make it into such a prestigious venue as the Smithsonian, she said. "I'm a serious artist, but not about getting recognition."

She even finds selling her beadwork — which she calls a very personal expression of her feelings — distasteful.

"I don't get excited about my art when it comes to letting other people see it. It's a personal thing," she said.

However, necessity forced her for several years to trade her beads for cash; first as part of the crafts entourage that follow the rock group the Grateful Dead on its tours, and then at arts fairs in Eugene.

Vinson's approach to selling her work is definitely anti-commercial. The intricate fringed neckpiece she had in the Smithsonian exhibit was sold, despite her best efforts to make it unmarketable by putting a steep price on it.

At arts fairs, she always shied away from customers, preferring to escape into her beadwork while friends handled transactions.

At one time, she opened a business, "And I failed miserably. Miserably."

Then she wrote a book on beadwork — she knows 60 to 70 stitches and the cultural background of each — but didn't know how to sell it.

Fortunately, her father-in-law is in marketing and offered to handle that aspect.

It was when Vinson learned the cultural significance of the stitches, which have names like African Flower Mandala and Comanche stitch, that she began viewing her work as an art rather than a craft.

"Something you and I would look at as a very pretty necklace is a symbol to somebody else of going to war. It's a warpiece," Vinson said.

She never jots down her design ideas, which come to her in her sleep and which she can only describe as feelings. "They're feelings, they're not pictures. I know that sounds weird.

"I can't sit down and plan a piece. It takes the fun out of it."

For now, her beadwork is on hold while Sean is still young. Beadwork "focuses me," Vinson said. "I get lost in it, which is probably why I'm not doing it because everything else falls by the wayside: the house, the child."

Vinson, whose family relocated to upstate New York when she was eight months old, left an abusive home at 14 to live in New York City, she later toured with the Dead for five years, then moved to Eugene in 1985.

She met husband Greg — a music teacher at both the Wamic and Maupin elementary schools and Wasco Union High School — when both were students in Eugene. They and their son Sean moved to Maupin in 1990.

Vinson has always loved to work with her hands. "I was the child who took the clock apart and then tried to figure *how* I took it apart — before my parents got home.

"The riding lawn mower my father was really proud of? I dismantled it."

Now she has her own child, who has taught her a few important beadwork lessons, like never doing the painstaking work in a carpeted room.

That pointer was learned after Sean overturned a tray of minuscule beads, which were promptly swallowed up by the carpet.

"Real picky" about her work, Vinson has shoeboxes full of halfway done pieces that she's abandoned or temporarily set aside. "I can't rush them. It's almost like doing a painting."

She prefers beads in greens, purples and blues and favors the stitches of African and South American cultures.

She buys her beads in bulk, to avert her biggest fear: running out of a unique color halfway through a piece — beads are made by dye lot and no two lots are the same.

While she can do earrings in a half hour, and a necklace in anywhere from a hour to three days, her major piece of beadwork now is a green and silver waistpiece, which has been in the works for two years.

She anticipates it will be another three years before she finishes it.

While Vinson is comfortable saying her work is good, mostly because others have told her it is, she believes it is an art anyone can master.

But, she concedes in understatement, "It takes a lot of patience."